Mercer University, Law School, Macon, Georgia, 15 September 1986.

FLORIDA STATE
UNIVERSITY LIBRARIES

MAR 14 1994

TALLAHASSEE, FLORIDA

GEORGE

George Waldo Woodruff

Waldo Woodruff

A Life of Quiet Achievement

DELLA WAGER WELLS

ISBN 0-86554-298-8

HC
102.5
W66
W45
1987

George Woodruff
Copyright © 1987 by Mercer University
All rights reserved
Printed in the United States of America

Library of Congress Cataloging-in-Publication Data
Wells, Della Wager.
George Waldo Woodruff : a life of quiet achievment.
Includes index.
1. Woodruff, George Waldo. 2. Businessmen—United
States—Biography. 3. Engineers—United States—Biography.
4. Philanthropists—United States—Biography.
I. Title.
HC102.5.W66W45   1987   338'.04'0924 [B]   87-24700
ISBN 0-86554-298-8

Contents

Preface — vii

Chapter One
Origins in Industry — 1

Chapter Two
Growing Up With a City — 15

Chapter Three
An Epistolary Romance — 43

Chapter Four
From Turmoil to Tranquility — 69

Chapter Five
An Industrious Citizen — 97

Epilogue — 157

Index — 159

for Jere

Preface

This biography is the story of a life that is more notable for the consistency of its goodness, honesty, and integrity than it is for any single instance of glory or isolated achievement. George Waldo Woodruff was a man of quiet strength and dedication to duty, and as I interviewed numbers of his business associates, friends, and family members, a clear picture emerged of an individual of unshakable faith, unswerving loyalty, and steady generosity who was regarded with both respect and affection. George Woodruff was a man who, in making large financial contributions and commitments of support in his habitually modest and unassuming manner, was a substantial force for good, and his humility made his magnanimity all the more worthy of emulation.

In researching and writing this biography of Mr. George, the greatest privilege was coming to know the man himself as we sat for many hours in his home and office talking about his life. His warm handshake and twinkling eyes were sincere greetings and will always stand out as fond memories for me. He told stories of his achievements with understatement and a total lack of embroidery—any details on the magnitude of his giving or the extent of his advisory involvement in different corporations and organizations had to come from other sources.

This book could not have come together without the efforts and cooperation of many people, and help from all quarters was eagerly given. Those who were close to Mr. George, Vela Rocker, Nita Broschat, Cody Dowling, Ted Kuzy, and, most importantly, his daughter, Jane Woodruff, and his granddaughter, Missie Raudabaugh, I thank for their help and continuing warm friendship. The presidents of the various institutions in which Mr. George had been interested, Dr. R. Kirby Godsey of Mercer University, Dr. James T. Laney of Emory University, Mr. Donn M. Gaebelein of The Westminster Schools, Dr. Ruth Schmidt of Agnes Scott College, the late Dr. Joseph M. Pettit of Georgia Tech, and Dr. Karl Anderson, former headmaster of Rabun Gap-Nacoochee School, were all generous with their time and personal recollections of Mr. Woodruff's participation in their schools' affairs.

I am indebted to the Atlanta Historical Society for its vast resources, both archival and human. I especially thank the ever-cheerful, always innovative and willing Anne Salter, Nancy Wight, Don Rooney, Bill Hull, and Elaine Kirkland for their collective diligence and competence. Billy Howard at Emory University's Photographic Services is due credit for the photograph of Mr. George on the dust jacket, while Elizabeth Drinnon of Mercer University gathered together Mercer's full collection of photographs of Mr. Woodruff, many of them taken by Mercer photographer Judy Lunsford, and Judy then took the photograph of Mr. Woodruff and me working together in his office in the Trust Company that appears on the back flap of the dustjacket. Emily Myers, Vice President for Development at Mercer, was tremendously helpful with information and logistics and was also the person who conceived of this book.

John A. Sibley was able to read the first two chapters of this biography in draft form very shortly before his death on October 25, 1986, and my extreme respect and affection for him, when combined with his great knowledge through lifelong friendship and business association with Mr. Woodruff, made his pronouncement that those chapters were "good characterizations of George" the most effective encouragement I could have received.

I thank Yvonne McMillian for looking after me at the office for all of these years, Susie Harman for transcribing hours of interviews, Dave Shores for bridging the gap between scholarship and technology by making sense of Chapter Five's footnotes on the computer, and Jayné LaMondue-Price for picking up the pieces. Lastly, I thank Bob Steed—for his editorial assistance, advice, friendship, and considerable encouragement to finish this project.

DELLA WAGER WELLS
Atlanta 1987

Chapter One

Origins in Industry

On August 27, 1985, George Waldo Woodruff stood before an assembly of about 350 well-wishers, preparing to speak. The crowd he gazed out over included people of all ages, from many walks of life. There were friends from his youth, fellow board members from major corporations, presidents and officers of renowned educational institutions, lawyers, bankers, politicians, and students, who, although they did not personally know the man standing before them, were well aware of his influence on the educational facilities at their schools. The crowd sat. Quiet and expectant, they waited for the guest of honor to speak.

"Thank you, God, for letting me live to be ninety years old," Woodruff began in a strong voice. "I am overwhelmed by this celebration. . . . I have attended many birthday celebrations in my ninety years, but I have never attended one of such magnitude as this. As I look out over this gathering, I see the faces of scores of men and women from various companies and institutions whose hard work and outstanding accomplishments through the years have made it possible for me to do all that I have done. So you see, in reality, it is I who am indebted to you."[1]

George W. Woodruff, businessman, industrialist, mechanical engineer, philanthropist, son, father, husband, and friend, was deeply moved by his well-wishers' expressions of affection and appreciation, but responded with characteristic humility to their outpourings of praise. Although Woodruff was born and raised in an environment of great privilege, he was known throughout his life as a man of simple needs and tastes. Family and friends, rather than ambitions, were the driving forces in his life, and although he had vast financial means and was responsible for gifts of staggering sums to many worthwhile educational, medical, and cultural causes, he was unimpressed by the financial influence he wielded and studiously avoided recognition for his role in various benefactions until his very advanced years. While Woodruff was justifiably proud of his family's great heritage and fortune, he placed a much greater emphasis on his own ability to measure up to personally set standards of honesty and integrity. Merely to bask in the history of an impressive lineage, Woodruff felt, was inexcusable. A man should focus on the worth of his own acts and character as a source of his self-esteem.

While Woodruff did believe strongly in meeting personally set standards and judging himself on his own merits and reputation, it is impossible to tell the story of his life without reference to those who came before him and walked with him. His family had for many generations been steeped in traditions of hard work and involvement in civic and charitable affairs. It is apparent from early records of Woodruff's ancestors that business success and community responsibility were expectations. A genealogy prepared for the family traces George Woodruff's lineage back to Matthew Woodruff of Farmington, Connecticut, who bought several acres of land from two of Farmington's original proprietors in 1653. It is with this early ancestor that existing records of Woodruff determination and industry begin. While there are no authenticated records that reveal the date of Matthew Woodruff's direct ancestors' arrival in the New World or even where Matthew himself lived prior to his purchase of land in Farmington, it is fairly certain that the family had its origins in England. Families with the name *Woodruff* were residents at early dates in the English shires of Oxford, Lincoln, Huntingdon, York, Surrey, Devon, and Kent. For the most part, they appear to have been British landed gentry and yeomanry, a class of English freeholders below the gentry.[2]

The name *Woodruff*, like many other surnames, probably was derived from the trade of an early family member. While spelling of the name varied widely from Woodrove, Woodrough, and Woodroffe through Woodrow, Woodrue, and Woodrof to finally become Woodruff, the names probably all referred to a wood-reeve, a minor English official who served as a kind of forest warden or wood-bailiff. A fanciful but perhaps less credible explanation of the name's origin is that "woodruff" was a common herb used extensively in England as a perfume. People would carry the sweet-smelling herb in their prayerbooks, and the scent was so strong that it would cling to them, earning them the nickname *Woodruff*.[3]

Whatever the origin of the name, the family is most likely of Anglo-Saxon descent, and there are records of Woodruffs in the earliest days of England, although George Woodruff's direct line of descent from those individuals has not been confirmed. John Woderove of Oxford is one of the first to be noted in 1273, and Robert Woderoue of Huntingdonshire is recorded around the same time. Another John, who spelled his name variously as Woodroffe and Woodroufe, lived in Devonshire in the sixteenth century. His son David was the first sheriff of London in 1554, and David's son, Sir Nicholson Woodroffe, was the first Lord Mayor of London in 1574.

While it is certainly possible that George Woodruff's line of descent begins as thus charted in thirteenth century England, the first verified link in the Woodruff chain is Matthew Woodruff of Farmington, a small community not far from Hartford, Connecticut, then seat of government for the Colony of Connecticut. The Farmington community was settled after some men from Hartford, curious to know what lay beyond the hills to the west of their community, explored the area and returned with descriptions of the green valley of the Tunxis River, perfect for their plan of cattle breeding.[4] Settlement began in 1640. The community, originally called "Tunxis" after Uncas ("Tunxis") Sepos, an Indian leader, was chartered as Farmington in 1645, although at that time, the proprietors' rights rested upon a relatively informal agreement with Sequasson, the chief of the neighboring Indian tribes. In 1685, however, the year James II of England acceded to the throne, the proprietors applied to the legislature of the Commonwealth of Connecticut and a patent was granted, formally confirming the 1645 grant. The names of Matthew Woodruff and his eldest son, John, appear among the forty-three original settlers who came to the community as early as 1640.

While the community continued to grow over those early years, life was not easy. The eighty-four proprietors counted in 1672 had survived harsh conditions, both natural and human. The winters were long and difficult, and the community was in the midst of large, hostile tribes of Indians, including the most feared, Mohawks, who had their territory not far to the west of the Farmington settlement. The settlers overcame the difficulties, however, and the community prospered. The Woodruffs became members of the church in town, and in 1672, Matthew Woodruff was made a constable of Farmington. After serving in that capacity for some years, Matthew Woodruff died in 1682 at the age of seventy.

While it is unclear whether Matthew was married at the time he arrived in Farmington in the 1640s, it is recorded that his children were born there. Matthew married a woman by the name of Hannah, and their youngest son, Samuel, was born in Farmington in 1661. Samuel married Rebecca Clark, a Farmington woman, and soon after was appointed sealer of weights and measures for Farmington. Samuel and Rebecca lived in Farmington until the birth of their son Daniel, sixth of their twelve children, in 1696. They then moved to the south part of town, later named Southington, where they were the first white settlers. The Wongonk Indians' camp was a mile downstream from the family's homestead, and Samuel Woodruff was known for being on good terms with them throughout his life. He is reputed to have been an excellent hunter and trapper, and it is local legend that after Hannah's death in 1737, Samuel enjoyed several seasons camping with the nearby friendly Indians before his death in Southington in 1742 at the age of eighty-one.

Samuel and Rebecca's sixth child, Daniel, married Lydia Smith, daughter of Ephraim and Rachel Cole Smith. Daniel was an ensign in Southington's small military company, and he and Lydia had six children, with their eldest, Jonathan, born in 1720. Daniel died at eighty-nine and Lydia at ninety-nine in Southington, and they were buried in Oak Hill Cemetery there. Their son Jonathan married Phebe Wiard, the daughter of John and Phebe Hurlbut Wiard of Weathersfield, Connecticut. Jonathan and Phebe lived east of Southington and begat nine children, the eighth of whom, Ashbel, was born in 1761. Jonathan and Phebe both died in 1782 in Southington, and their son Ashbel married Sybil Ingraham of Bristol, Connecticut, in 1795. The couple had five children, with their second child, George Wyllys, born in 1800 in the Flanders district of Southington. Ashbel died in Southington in 1836 at the age of seventy-five, while Sybil survived him by nineteen years, dying in 1855 at the age of eighty-four.

George Wyllys Woodruff, the son of Ashbel and Phebe, was the first in five generations of Woodruffs to leave the Farmington and Southington area, and it is his adventuresome spirit that brought the Woodruff family to Georgia. In 1822, he married Lucy Mesherel, the daughter of John and Polly Smith Mesherel, in Southington. George and Lucy Woodruff had five children in the ten years they were married before Lucy's death in September of 1832. George, left alone with two sons and three daughters, all under nine years old, almost immediately married Diadamia Dunham, the daughter of Samuel and Lucy Ariail Dunham. The marriage has been characterized as unfortunate, as Diadamia, the new Mrs. Woodruff, was a somewhat ill-tempered schoolmarm who, although she was fond of little girls, disliked boys intensely and mistreated them.[5] After assessing the situation, George Wyllys Woodruff took action. Within months of their marriage, Woodruff took his sons, George Waldo, then eight, and Charles Henry, two, with him to Smokey Ordinary, Virginia, leaving all of his properties with his daughters, Jane, Lucy, and Alzara, and his new wife in Southington.

George Wyllys Woodruff remained in Virginia long enough for his sons to receive their grammar school level education before moving on to Macon, Georgia. In Macon, the elder Woodruff owned a store, and his son George spent his teen years clerking there. After several years in Macon, the three Woodruff men moved on to Columbus, Georgia, arriving in 1842, when George Waldo was eighteen. There George Wyllys opened another store, and George Waldo resumed clerking, although legend has it that his sense of filial duty was so strong that he never expected or received any payment for his services.[6] This relationship continued until 1848, when George Waldo formed a partnership with a Mr. Merry in Columbus and began operating what was to become a very profitable clothing store. Around that time, with his older son engaged in a successful business, George Wyllys decided to return to his home in Southington, Connecticut, accompanied by his younger son, Charles Henry, after an absence of sixteen years. Joy at the elder Woodruff's homecoming was short-lived, however, as he died within a year of his return on December 29, 1849, at the age of forty-nine.

From the perspective of the Woodruff family's great generosity to Georgia and the southern region, George Wyllys Woodruff's ill-advised marriage and resultant hasty retreat with his two sons were fortuitous events. Without such strange goings-on, the Woodruff family might never have been induced to leave Connecticut, and the great financial and industrial advances that the southern region has witnessed in part through their efforts could well have suffered without their contributions and labors. George Wyllys Woodruff's sojourn in the South, however, had a significant result: after his return home to Connecticut, son George Waldo Woodruff remained in Columbus and continued to prosper.

On April 23, 1850, eight years after his arrival in Columbus, George Waldo Woodruff married Virginia Bright Lindsay, the daughter of Sherwood Conner Lindsay and Elizabeth Bright Cooper Lindsay of Columbus.[7] The Lindsays had been a prominent old North Carolina family before their 1840 move to Columbus, Georgia, where they continued in affluence, operating a successful plantation.[8] The family mansion on the plantation, Sherwood Hall, provided an elegant setting for the wedding of George and Virginia, especially when compared to the cottage on the Lindsay plantation where they lived after the wedding. "Hard Bargain," their tiny home, had been built by Virginia's father as a place for each of his children to spend their first year of married life.

George and Virginia Woodruff had their first two children while living in Columbus, with Henry Lindsay born at "Hard Bargain" in 1851 and George Sherwood at the family's home in 1852. In 1853, George Waldo Woodruff moved his young family to Juniper, Georgia, where he formed a partnership with a Mr. Goetchius to run a sawmill business. Although their enterprise was very successful, George Woodruff left the partnership after six years to return to Columbus with his family, which had been enlarged in 1854 and 1855 by the arrivals of daughters Virginia Lee and Annie Bright Woodruff. In Columbus, he joined in forming Browne, Woodruff & Clements, a partnership planned to continue in the sawmill business on a broader scale. That same year, 1859, the partnership established Empire Mills, the business that was ultimately to earn George Waldo Woodruff the greatest part of his fortune.[9]

By the time the Civil War began in 1861, Empire Mills was a great success. Unfortunately, Woodruff's confidence in both the certainty of his investment and the strength of his region was so great that through the course of the war he kept all of his wealth in Confederate currency, except for ten dollars in gold. At the war's end, however, even with the South defeated, the mill itself destroyed in Sherman's march, and almost his entire fortune gone, Woodruff rallied. He borrowed enough money from friends to buy one freight car load of corn and another of wheat and persuaded one of his former partners, Mr. Browne, to repair the ruined mill on credit. Woodruff began production again with great success, ultimately amassing a fortune greater than the one he had lost.[10]

While the Civil War was raging, two more sons had been born to the Woodruff family—Ernest Woodruff in 1863, and Francis Wood-

George Waldo Woodruff (1824-1911), husband of Virginia Woodruff, father of Ernest Woodruff, and grandfather of George W. Woodruff.

Virgina Lindsay Woodruff (1830-1911), wife of the elder George W. Woodruff, mother of Earnest Woodruff, and grandmother of George W. Woodruff

ruff in 1865. Francis, George and Virginia Woodruff's lastborn child, died at the age of two in 1867, but Ernest thrived, displaying all of his father's and grandfather's most valuable business instincts.[11] The same sharp mind and determination that had allowed George Wyllys Woodruff to open a successful mercantile establishment with very little capital and George Waldo Woodruff to rebuild a war-ravaged mill with almost no capital was present with a vengeance in young Ernest.

After finishing public school and business college in Columbus in 1883 at about the age of twenty, Ernest Woodruff started modestly, working as a salesman for his father's Empire Mills in a territory that covered an appreciable portion of west Georgia and east Alabama.[12] Traveling by horse and buggy, he would go off for a week at a time on his selling trips, taking orders for flour from stores, boarding houses, and individual households. Because of the limited size of the buggy, deliveries were made at a later date, usually by another employee. While he was on the road, Woodruff most often stayed in boarding houses, as hotels were scarce in the nearly 1880s, particularly in the small towns he visited. Despite the relative unavailability

Emily Caroline Winship Woodruff (1867-1939), mother of George W. Woodruff, taken in about 1885.

Ernest Woodruff (1863-1944), father of George W. Woodruff, taken in about 1885.

of accommodations as present day business travelers know them, a salesman traveling by horse and buggy was not an odd sight in those days. Many home products such as milk, produce, bread, flour, sugar, and other bulk goods were sold door to door.[13]

Not long after beginning work as a flour salesman for his father, Ernest Woodruff married Emily Caroline Winship, the daughter of Robert and Mary Frances Overby Winship of Atlanta. The couple met through Ernest's older sister Annie Bright Woodruff, who had married Atlantan Joel Hurt in 1876. On one of his visits to his sister and brother-in-law's home, Ernest became acquainted with Emily Winship, who lived next door to the Hurts on Spring Street with her parents. Emily and Ernest were married on April 22, 1885, at the Winship home.[14]

The Winship family, like the Woodruff family, has a long and distinguished heritage. Genealogists have traced the Winship line back to the days of Queen Elizabeth I of England, although the first Winship did not arrive in the New World until 1634, fourteen years after the landing of the *Mayflower*. Edward Winship, born in 1611 in

Newcastle, crossed the Atlantic on the ship *Defence* and settled in Cambridge, Massachusetts, where he became a large landholder and attained a position of great social prominence.[15] In 1638, Edward became a member of the Ancient and Honorable Artillery Company in Cambridge. He was commissioned as an ensign in that company in 1647 and became Lieutenant of the Militia in 1660. During his lifetime he also served as a Selectman in Massachusetts for fourteen years and a Representative for six. He and his wife Elizabeth had thirteen children and lived out their lives in Cambridge, where Edward died in 1688. Elizabeth's death is unrecorded.

Edward Winship II, Edward and Elizabeth's eighth child, also served as a Selectman for many years in Massachusetts and was an officer in the Cambridge Company in King Philip's War of 1675. He married Rebecca Barsham, and they had six children and lived out their lives in Cambridge, where Rebecca died in 1717 and Edward's death followed the next year. They were buried in the churchyard opposite the entrance to Harvard University.

Edward and Rebecca's eldest son, also named Edward, was born in Cambridge in 1684 and held many minor offices in government. He married Sarah Manning in 1705, and the couple had seven children, the youngest of whom, Isaac, was born in 1724. While there is no record of Sarah's death, Edward Winship III died in Lexington, Massachusetts, in 1763 at the age of ninety-nine.

Isaac, Edward and Sarah's lastborn child, served in both the French and Indian and the Revolutionary Wars, married Hannah, whose surname is unrecorded, and with her produced thirteen children. Isaac and Hannah's eleventh child, Benjamin, was born in 1766 in Lexington, Massachusetts, where Isaac died in 1783. Benjamin owned and operated a large farm near New Salem, Massachusetts, and he and his wife, Mary Adams Winship, had six children. Their second child, Joseph, was born on the family's plantation and spent most of his early life there. As a young man, he became apprenticed to a maker of boots and shoes, and when his employer announced plans to move south, the young Joseph Winship decided to follow him. They ended up in Georgia, where Joseph soon met and married Emily Hutchings, the daughter of Robert and Drucella Bonner Hutchings and a direct descendant of the Wyatt family of England, who could trace her lineage back to 919 A.D. The Wyatt family was of English royal heritage and first arrived in the New World in the early 1600s, where the brother of Emily Hutchings Winship's great-great-great-great grandfather, Sir Frances Wyatt, was governor of the colony of Virginia for extended periods of time between 1621 and 1642.

Joseph Winship and his employer first opened for business in Monticello, Georgia, but moved after two years to Jones County. From Jones County, they moved on to Clinton, and from there, Joseph Winship went on alone to Forsyth, where he established a factory and tannery in partnership with his brother Isaac, who had also decided to migrate south. Shortly after opening the factory and tannery in Forsyth, Joseph sold out his interest to Isaac and went back into business as a merchant in Clinton. In 1845, he closed his store and established a cotton gin factory in Morgan County, which he operated successfully until around 1851. At that time, he turned over the management and ownership of the factory to his two sons-in-law and moved on to Atlanta, where he began manufacturing freight cars on the site that is now 10 Forsyth Street. As his business expanded, it became necessary for Joseph Winship to start an iron foundry to supply his needs for the manufacture of the freight cars, so in partnership with his brother Isaac, he built a foundry further down the Western and Atlantic Railroad line on the site where the Omni now stands, and the resulting extensive plant ultimately became known as the Winship Machine Works.[16] When the freight car factory was destroyed by fire in 1856, Winship decided to focus his attention on the iron works instead of rebuilding, and he took his two sons, Robert and George, into partnership with him at that time, doing business as Joseph Winship & Sons.

During the Civil War, the Winship Machine Company supported the Confederate cause by producing guns and other military supplies until General Sherman's march brought about the foundry's destruction in 1864.[17] At the war's end, however, the company again began to prosper as Isaac Winship sold out his interest in the business and moved to Macon while Robert and George Winship, Joseph's sons, took over the greater part of the company's managerial responsibilities. Joseph Winship retired fully in 1873, and his sons carried on the business under the name of Winship & Brother.[18] In 1878, Joseph died at the age of seventy-eight, and seven years later, the brothers decided to incorporate the company as the Winship Machine Company. They elected George Winship as president, Robert Winship as vice-president, and Robert E. Rushton as secretary, and for the remaining fourteen years before the newly incorporated firm merged with six other cotton gin manufacturers to form the Continental Gin Company, the Winship Machine Company was known as one of the most important industries in Atlanta.[19]

Robert Winship, fifth of Joseph and Emily Hutchings Winship's eleven children, was born in 1834 in Forsyth, Georgia. He attended schools in Jones and Morgan counties until coming to Atlanta with his father and younger brother George when he was about eighteen. In 1860, about four years after he became a partner in the firm of Joseph Winship & Sons, he married Mary Frances Overby, the daughter of Basil Hallum and Asenath Caroline Thrasher Overby of Atlanta. Basil Overby was one of the most distinguished lawyers in Georgia at that time and had run a vigorous but ultimately unsuccessful campaign as the Prohibition candidate for governor in 1855. Their third of seven children, Mary Frances, started out her married life with Robert Winship in a house on Spring Street, on the site where the Greyhound Bus Station now stands.[20] Their first child,

Mary Frances Overby Winship (1842-1915), wife of Robert Winship, mother of Emily Winship Woodruff, and grandmother of George W. Woodruff. George and Irene Woodruff's second child was her namesake.

Robert Winship (1834-1899), husband of Mary Frances Winship, father of Emily Winship, and grandfather of George W. Woodruff. Winship established the Winship Machine Company with his father and brother in Atlanta in the 1850s. The Winship Machine Company was ultimately merged with five other companies in 1899 to form the Continental Gin Company.

Charles Robert, was born in 1863 and was his uncle's successor as president of the Winship Machine Company. Emily Caroline Winship, the second of the couple's five children, was born in 1867, and Maria Elizabeth and Mary Frances followed in 1872 and 1877. The Winships' youngest daughter, Anne, died in infancy.

Ernest and Emily Woodruff lived for the first eight years of their marriage in Columbus, where they had their first two children, Robert Winship in 1889 and Ernest in 1893. By the time his second son and namesake was born, Ernest Woodruff had been working with his father at the Empire Mills for ten years and had enjoyed great success, rising from salesman to vice president of the mill.[21] Two months after Grover Cleveland took office, however, the gold panic of 1893 gripped the country and ushered in a prolonged period of economic depression. While the Empire Mills were not crippled by the hard times that led to bankruptcies, unemployment, and reduced wages all over the United States, the atmosphere of financial tension was sufficient to render Ernest Woodruff amenable to his brother-in-law Joel Hurt's suggestion that he move his family to Atlanta. Agreeing with his brother-in-law that Atlanta held a greater variety of business opportunities, Woodruff accepted Hurt's offer of positions with his then pet projects, the Atlanta Consolidated Street Railway Company and the Commercial Travelers Savings Bank, precursor of the Trust Company of Georgia. Ernest Woodruff then moved his young family to Atlanta, where they lived in a home owned by his father on Euclid Avenue, near the center of Inman Park.[22]

It was in this small house on Euclid Avenue that George Waldo Woodruff, third son of Emily and Ernest Woodruff and a member of the eighth generation of Woodruffs on American soil, was born on August 27, 1895. The young George Woodruff, while named for his paternal grandfather, stepped into more than just the first George Waldo Woodruff's legacy of keen business sense, strong faith, and devotion to the welfare of the community. Woodruff's inheritance of these personal assets came over the centuries, from both his mother's and his father's side of the family, and were far more valuable than mere financial wealth. With tradition standing behind him and his family standing with him, the stage was set for young George Waldo Woodruff to face the expectations of his birthright.

ENDNOTES

[1]From speech notes of George W. Woodruff, 27 August 1985, available in Woodruff's personal files.

[2]*The Genealogy of the Robert Winship Woodruff Family*, comp. Lucille Huffman (Atlanta: The Coca-Cola Company, 1973) 1-55. I am indebted to this source for the genealogical information that follows unless otherwise noted.

[3]*The Pensacola Journal*, Pensacola, Florida, "What's in Your Name?" 27 September 1967.

[4]The Tunxis River is now known as the West Branch of the Farmington River.

[5]Sarah Simms Edge, *Joel Hurt and the Development of Atlanta* (Atlanta: The Atlanta Historical Society, 1955) 51.

[6]Ibid., 54.

[7]*The Columbus Enquirer,* "George W. Woodruff, Pioneer and Wealthy Citizen Passes Away," 5 November 1911.

[8]Edge, *Joel Hurt,* quoting a newspaper article entitled "Sketches and Pictures of Famous Historic Mansions," found in scrapbook of Annie Bright Woodruff Hurt, daughter of Virginia Bright Lindsay Woodruff.

[9]Ibid., 55, 57.

[10]George W. Woodruff obituary.

[11]Huffman, *Genealogy,* 9.

[12]Kenneth Coleman and Charles Stephen Gurr, eds., *Dictionary of Georgia Biography,* Vol. II, (Athens, Georgia: University of Georgia Press, 1983) 1083-1085.

[13]Personal interview with George W. Woodruff, 20 May 1986.

[14]Edge, *Joel Hurt,* 62-63, 115.

[15]Huffman, *Genealogy,* 24-25. I am indebted to this source for the genealogy that follows unless otherwise noted.

[16]Ibid.

Woodruff interview, 20 May 1986.

[17]*The Atlanta Journal*, "Robert Winship Died Yesterday," 9 September 1899.

[18]Ibid.

[19]Robert E. Rushton, secretary of the Winship Machine Company, was Irene Woodruff King's maternal grandfather (personal interview with George W. Woodruff, 20 May 1986).

[20]Woodruff interview, 20 May 1986.

[21]"Ernest Woodruff" in *Who's Who in America: A Biographical Dictionary of Notable Living Men and Women of the United States, Vol. 19, 1936-1937, Two Years,* Albert Nelson Marquis, ed. (Chicago: A. N. Marquis Company, 1936) 2658.

[22]Edge, *Joel Hurt,* 116.

Chapter Two
Growing Up With A City

Eighteen ninety-five, the year of George W. Woodruff's birth, was a formative year for the City of Atlanta. While many of the city's great institutions, including The Coca-Cola Company and the Trust Company of Georgia, had already been founded, an event took place that year that brought unprecedented waves of people to Atlanta, laying the groundwork for still more new industry and growth. In 1881, Atlanta had hosted the International Cotton Exposition, a kind of industrial fair that showcased the city's and the region's development as a trade, transportation, distribution, and manufacturing center. The 1881 exposition drew new residents to Atlanta in droves with the promise that the city was indeed, as *Atlanta Constitution* editor Henry W. Grady had begun to call it, the progressive and prosperous capital of the New South.

In 1895, wishing to repeat and expand on the success of the 1881 exposition, city leaders began to promote a second cotton exhibition along the same lines as the first, but on a much grander scale, with a longer run, more extensive grounds, and many more exhibits. The promoters, known as the Piedmont Exposition Company, secured the grounds that now comprise Piedmont Park with the help of the newly formed Gentlemen's Driving Club, later renamed the Piedmont Driving Club, and began to build roads and clear the hollow for Lake Clara Meer.[1]

The Cotton States and International Exposition, as the event was called, exceeded all of its planners' expectations in bringing national and international attention to Atlanta. Opening on time on September 18, 1895, the Exposition boasted 6,000 exhibits, 800,000 visitors within the first ten days, and 55,000 people on Atlanta Day alone—a number equal to about three-fourths of the city's population. Visitors converged on Atlanta from all states and countries, and scores of public officials, including President Grover Cleveland and thirty-five United States governors, toured the grounds at various times.[2] Exhibits highlighted inventions and technological achieve-

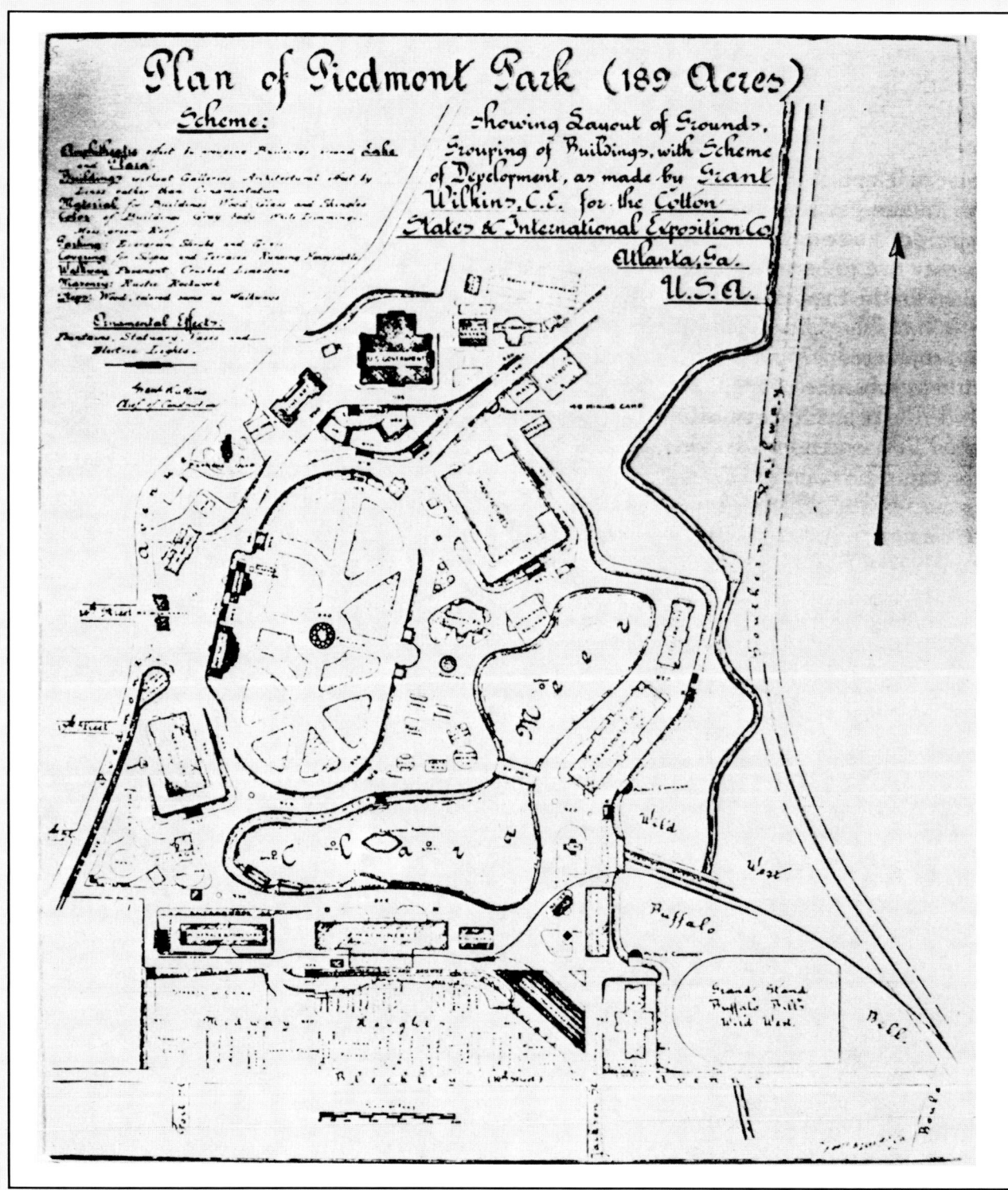

A map showing the locations of buildings and other attractions at Piedmont Park during the Cotton States and International Exposition, September 18-December 31, 1895. From the official catalogue of the Exposition. Notice Buffalo Bill's West Exhibit at the bottom right corner. (Courtesy of the Atlanta Historical Society.)

ments in industry, transportation, forestry, and agriculture, and the entertainment available ranged from an interesting but largely unsuccessful moving picture to Buffalo Bill's Wild West Show and Trilby of the Midway, perhaps the earliest burlesque dancer to reach Atlanta. More than 3,500 editors and reporters from twenty-six different state press associations visited the Exposition during its three-month run, writing over 100,000 articles in ten different languages that were printed and circulated all over the world.[3]

On August 27, 1895, in the midst of the great hubbub of activity surrounding the Cotton States and International Exposition, George Waldo Woodruff was born. Any effects of the gold panic of 1893 that did reach Atlanta had abated, and the collective mood of the city's planners was expansive—pro-development and more than ready for growth and challenge. As a child born into an advantaged family and a fertile economic climate, Woodruff enjoyed the most salutary effects of both nature and nurture. In addition to his impressive heritage of financial success and civic responsibility, Woodruff also was nurtured from birth in an atmosphere of prosperity, receiving education by example in the midst of his father's and extended family's remarkable business acumen. His childhood in Inman Park was happy and active, spent surrounded by friends, family, and strong codes of discipline. His parents were the most direct influences in his early life, and he was extremely close to both of them. Ernest Woodruff, although often characterized by his sons, friends, and acquaintances as a stern and exacting man, emerges in correspondence between himself and his son as a loving, affectionate parent. Of his father, George Woodruff later said simply, "I had great respect for him, and I loved him."[4]

Emily Winship Woodruff has also often been misleadingly cast by those describing her in print and oral legend. While she is most often noted for her sweetness and her generous spirit, she also had a personal strength and integrity that were equally prominent and influential components of her character. She was, as George Woodruff later described her, "a wonderful mother," who felt very strongly that while her sons were young, her duty was to her husband, children, and home, and she avoided women's social organizations and civic involvements during that period in her life. Emily Woodruff was, in short, "not a clubwoman at all."[5] Her avoidance of outside distractions carried over into her Sunday life as well. While she attended the Inman Park Methodist Church with her family every Sunday, she did not commit her time to any of the missionary societies that were popular among women of that period. Instead, she shepherded her family down Edgewood Avenue each week, picking up her mother, Mary Frances Winship, on the way, to be certain that Sunday worship was a family experience.[6] George Woodruff inherited her strong faith and became a member of the Inman Park Methodist Church soon after his sixth birthday, attending until he went away to college. When he married Irene Tift King at the age of twenty-three, they joined the First Presbyterian Church and were members of that congregation throughout their lives.[7]

George W. Woodruff as an infant.

In 1893, when, at Joel Hurt's suggestion, Ernest Woodruff moved his family to Atlanta from Columbus, there were two young Woodruff sons: Robert Winship and Ernest, Jr., who had been born in 1889 and 1893 respectively in Columbus. In 1895, George Waldo was born and named for his paternal grandfather in the family's house at 56 Euclid Avenue, which still stands today, although the street address was changed to 882 Euclid Avenue in 1927. In 1896, tragedy struck as young Ernest fell ill with spinal meningitis and died at the age of three, but the family again expanded to five the next year with the birth of Henry Francis Woodruff on November 14, 1897.

Although the three Woodruff sons were very close throughout their lives, they were just enough apart in age so that they didn't spend much time playing together as children. Robert, six years older than George, had his own friends in the neighborhood, some of the closest being his first cousins, Mabel and Eva Hurt. George and Henry each had his own neighborhood friends as well, but also played together with Mabel and Eva's youngest brother Sherwood, who was Henry's age. Some of George's and Henry's friends had horses, all

George W. Woodruff in about 1897, in then-traditional baby clothes.

(Credit: Kuhns-Atlanta)

horses, all had bicycles, and all enjoyed sandlot baseball and football after school and on Saturdays. Several of the boys, including George, Henry, and Sherwood, had goat wagons in addition to their bicycles, four-wheeled carts with traces for the goats, a seat, and room for two children in each wagon. Henry and Sherwood each had single-goat wagons, but George was very proud of his two-goat wagon and matched pair of goats which he, along with Sherwood and Henry, drove at a leisurely pace through Inman Park. "Goats aren't built to race," Woodruff later commented drily.[8]

George Woodruff attended the Edgewood Avenue School, still standing today as the Inman Park School, for the first eight years of his academic career. Walking the mile between his family's new home on Edgewood Avenue and the school four times a day, he would sometimes stop to visit briefly with his grandmother Winship, known to the Woodruff children as "Monie," who watched him faithfully from the window of her Edgewood Avenue home as he passed. Although George was close to his grandmother and grew up seeing a great deal of her, he had very little memory of his grandfather, Rob-

George W. Woodruff in sailor costume, taken in about 1899 at the age of four.

(Credit: Condon-Atlanta)

ther, Robert Winship, who had died in 1899 when George was four. Described in a newspaper account of his final illness as "one of the best known, wealthiest and most highly esteemed citizens of Atlanta," Robert Winship died at the relatively young age of sixty-five, and George Woodruff had a vivid memory of his grandmother's beautiful pair of grey horses and the carriage in which she drove to Oakland Cemetery every day to visit his grave.[9]

At Edgewood Avenue School, Woodruff studied the usual primary and middle school subjects—reading, writing, grammar, and arithmetic—without particular affection for any one of those disciplines. In eighth grade, however, he very much enjoyed the addition of science classes to his basic curriculum and applied himself with real interest. At Emily Woodruff's firm insistence, evenings were reserved for study. Dinner was served at sundown, and for the hours before bed, the Woodruff boys were expected to do their homework.[10]

When George Woodruff started at Edgewood Avenue School in around 1900, the Woodruff family had just moved from the Euclid Avenue house owned by George's paternal grandfather to a new house

Henry Woodruff, George W. Woodruff, and first cousin Sherwood Hurt in their three goat wagons in about 1907. The photograph was taken in front of the Woodruffs' Inman Park home at 708 Edgewood Avenue when George Woodruff was about twelve. The three boys enjoyed their wagons immensely, and George Woodruff was especially proud of his pair of goats. Woodruff's daughters later rode in a cart similar to this as children.

on the corner of Edgewood Avenue and Waverly Way that was designed and built for the family to Emily Woodruff's specifications in 1899 at a cost of approximately $20,000. The new house, erected at 708 Edgewood Avenue and designed by Atlanta architect Walter T. Downing, had a red brick exterior with a foundation of rough granite blocks. The pillars, pedestals, window frames, and balusters were crafted of light stone, and the house itself was in the English rustic style. The inside, in the somewhat fulsome words of a turn of the century Atlanta columnist, was "like a home in some modern fairyland with all those electrical furnishings that save so much time and effort. Mrs. Woodruff has only to touch certain buttons, turn little handles and knobs and behold the electric globes, bulbs, and blossoms burst into golden bloom, window shutters stand at attention, doors come open and servants come forward to receive commands."

Inman Park School, built in 1890 on Edgewood Avenue. George Woodruff walked to school from his parents' home at 708 Edgewood Avenue for eight years.

Home of Ernest and Emily Winship Woodruff at 908 Edgewood Avenue taken since the house's renovation in the late 1970s. Originally numbered 708 Edgewood, the house on the corner of Edgewood Avenue and Waverly Way in Inman Park was designed by local architect Walter T. Downing and built in 1899 at a cost of approximately $20,000. All three Woodruff sons grew up in this house. (Courtesy of the Atlanta Historical Society)

The porches were ornamented with Venetian mosaic floors, and all of the bathrooms were finished in marble. Downstairs, the house had a broad entrance hall decorated with carved Antwerp oak, a receiving room, two bedrooms, a butler's room, kitchen, china room, storage room, library, and dining room, where, the same reporter added rapturously, "[there was] a dear little noisy canary like a singing sunbeam."[11] A grand staircase with two landings led upstairs to four more bedrooms, and there was an exercise room in the basement furnished with parallel bars, a horse, and other fitness equipment for Ernest Woodruff and his sons.[12] The dining room, built to seat twenty-five guests, was the grandest room in the house, with the woodwork, mantel, sideboard, chairs, and table all made of Antwerp oak. Decorative electric lighting, innovative for the time, was the focal point of the room. Cut glass globes concealing electric light bulbs and candles lit by gas jets were installed around the perimeter of the red-walled room, and around the oval molding of the ceiling, the columnist effused, were "glass blossoms at intervals . . . in which electric globes burn like golden stamens in the hearts of wild roses."[13]

In his later years, George Woodruff recalled fondly the large back yard with stables for the family's horse and buggy, Robert's horse, Pat, and his own and Henry's goats. Also out back was a good sized vegetable garden, and the side yard held Emily Woodruff's flower garden, where she grew and bred all kinds of flowers and berries.[14] As a young boy with mechanical inclinations, George Woodruff was appreciative of the fineness and tasteful decor of his family home, but remembered the Edgewood Avenue house's technological innovations far more vividly. The family icebox, he later marveled, was especially built to hold the two hundred pound blocks of ice that were delivered to the house every other day by mule or horse and wagon at a time when the largest home iceboxes held only one hundred pounds of ice. Water from the melted ice drained out of the icebox under the house. The house also had hot water heat and a furnace that burned anthracite coal, both fairly new developments at the time the house was built.[15]

By the time that the Woodruff family built their new home in Inman Park in the late 1890s, the area had already begun to develop into one of the most desirable neighborhoods in the city. Robert and Mary Frances Winship, Emily Woodruff's parents, had built a home on Edgewood Avenue in about 1887, soon after the lots in Atlanta's first suburb had been put up for sale. Around the same time, Annie Bright and Joel Hurt, Ernest Woodruff's sister and brother-in-law and the Winships' former neighbors on Spring Street, moved to a small home on Elizabeth Street that had belonged to Hurt's cousin, Elizabeth Hurt Jones. She had owned the cottage and other property in the tiny village of Edgewood, which included the Inman Park area, and Hurt, who purchased all of her land to create Inman Park, named the first street he cut through the property in her honor.[16] After they had lived in the cottage for several years, the Hurts built a larger home for themselves at 85 Elizabeth Street, across Springvale Park from the Woodruffs' new Edgewood Avenue home.[17] An 1891 magazine article on Inman Park is evidence of Hurt's unique ability to see far into the future, as many of his selling points for the development are echoed by present day advertisements for subdivisions and planned residential communities:

The claims of Inman Park may be partially summed up as follows:
1. High location, with all of the essentials of healthfulness.
2. Proximity to the city—only two miles.
3. Rapid transit to and from business by the finest of electric railways—only a few minutes trip.
4. Superb society.
5. All of the surroundings of the beautiful and the ideal.[18]

Inman Park, an extremely elegant and beautifully landscaped early suburb, was only one of Joel Hurt's projects with which the Woodruff family became involved in one way or another. By the time Ernest Woodruff moved his family to Atlanta in 1893, Hurt had become a phenomenal business success in the city. After marrying Ernest's sister, Annie Bright, in 1876, his ascendence in the business world had led even Ernest's father, the elder George Woodruff, to invest frequently in Hurt's ventures, despite his lifelong reputation as a cautious businessman.[19] Hurt had an impressive sense of vision and a feeling for progress that was not daunted by apparent political, financial, or physical obstacles. He also had a reputation for conceiving of great enterprises or projects, getting them started, and then turning them over to others to continue or develop further.

It was this last characteristic of Hurt's that was especially fortuitous for Ernest Woodruff. When he arrived in Atlanta in 1893, Woodruff immediately was named vice president of the Atlanta Consolidated Street Railway, which Hurt had started in about 1889 to develop an electric street rail system in the city. At that time, Hurt was just beginning the process of planning Inman Park, and it was his goal to make the city's first suburb appealing to purchasers by emphasizing its proximity to the business district and the potential availability of transportation by streetrail from Inman Park to Five Points, then even more than now the hub of business and legal activity in Atlanta.

Joel Hurt (1850-1926) married Ernest Woodruff's sister Annie Bright at the family home in Columbus in 1876. It was Joel Hurt who convinced Ernest Woodruff to move his family to Atlanta from Columbus in 1893 and who involved him in many of his very lucrative business ventures.

Because Hurt saw the construction of an electric streetrail line as necessary to the success of both Inman Park and the downtown business district, where he had plans for commercial development, Hurt attacked the streetrail project with great energy. He tried out Georgia's first electric streetcar on Friday, August 21, 1889, on his Edgewood Street Railway Company line, which he, along with other investors, had chartered in 1886. The Edgewood Street Railway's charter provided for a line to run from the city into the little village of Edgewood via Inman Park. There was no roadway there at the time, and it was Hurt's plan to open a passage for the streetrail which he would ultimately landscape and develop to create what is now Edgewood Avenue.[20] The first run of the first streetcar was an enormous success, with between 20,000 and 30,000 spectators on hand to witness the miracle. Free rides were offered and accepted by the apprehensive but willing crowd, although many riders removed their watches and left them with bystanders, fearing that they would be "electrified."[21]

It was into this center of Joel Hurt's great enthusiasm that Ernest Woodruff stepped upon his arrival in Atlanta in 1893. Hurt had already begun buying up horse car lines in order to convert them to electricity and tie them into his own system, and he had purchased five hundred tons of steel rails in order to begin re-railing all of the old horse car lines in the city. He had also bought new cars, machinery, and electrical equipment to complete the renovation.[22] Additionally, Hurt had decided that electricity was a necessary adjunct to the street rail project, and accordingly had acquired an electric plant, the first in the city.[23]

The conjunction of electricity and street rails was the element that really made Ernest Woodruff's new job exciting, as Joel Hurt had by 1891 entered into a fierce competition with Harry M. Atkinson of Brookline, Massachusetts, with each trying to gain control of various street car lines and the electrical plants that would power them.[24] Ernest Woodruff, as vice president of the Atlanta Consolidated Street Railway Company, was a central figure in the contest that eventually involved many of the city's most prominent businessmen, politicians, lawyers, and newspapermen and has been characterized, only partly in jest, as "the Second Battle of Atlanta." Among other projects during Woodruff's tenure with the Consolidated was the process of linking the city's already existing street rail lines with its new routes, such as the one it built around 1894 from the center of Atlanta out to the Cotton States and International Exposition's grounds at Piedmont Avenue and 14th Street, then deep in the country.[25]

Ernest Woodruff continued as vice president of the Consolidated for four years, until Joel Hurt tendered his resignation as president of company in 1897 in order to devote more time to his other interests, most notably the Trust Company of Georgia. Ernest Woodruff was then named president of the Consolidated, and he continued in that capacity until the street car company and all of its electrical and street rail holdings, merged under the name Atlanta Railway & Power Company in 1899, were sold out to the competing Atkinson interests in 1901.[26] In his zealous representation of the Consolidated's interests, Woodruff consistently demonstrated the same keen business sense and talent for shrewd financial management that had distinguished his ancestors and would do the same for his sons. His role in the economic enthusiasm of Atlanta in the 1890s was nothing less than extraordinary, particularly for a man in his early to mid-thirties. In addition to his position with the Atlanta Consolidated Street Railway, he was also a director of the Trust Company of Georgia, which had just been formed from the Commercial Travelers Savings Bank through the infusion of new capital and great ambitions for Atlanta's growth.

George Woodruff grew up in the midst of his father's business ventures and gained an early sense of the responsibilities and hard work that go along with great financial success. While Ernest Woodruff did not discuss particular details of business matters with his family when his sons were young, they could not help but be aware of his connections to the Atlanta Consolidated Street Railway, Trust Company of Georgia, Atlantic Ice & Coal, and other projects he undertook. As a child, George sometimes accompanied his father to the car barn in Inman Park that housed equipment for the Atlanta Consolidated Street Railway, and he enjoyed looking at the cars there. He later noted with some humor, however, that despite his father's and his Uncle Joel Hurt's positions with the company, he and his cousin Sherwood Hurt, Joel's son, were not given any break on the nickel street car fare. Accordingly, the boys did not make special allowances to spare their fathers in their pranks—a particular favorite for George and Sherwood involved the Consolidated's street cars, which, conveniently enough, ran right by Sherwood's family's home in Inman Park. From each end of a street car hung a rope, which was attached to the electrical wire running overhead. For the car to go forward, the back mechanism had to be attached to the wire, and when the car reached the end of its route, the motorman would pull each rope, disconnecting the temporary "back" end of the car from the wire and connecting the other end, so that the car would then travel in the opposite direction. More than once, George and Sherwood found the rope trailing behind the streetcars far more temptation than little boys could resist and, running behind the car, would yank the trolley off the wire, bringing the disconnected streetcar to a sudden and unexpected halt. For this malfeasance, the cousins were "fussed at" by Uncle Joel, separated, and sent to their respective rooms.[27]

Another frequent outing that George Woodruff remembers was downtown to the Trust Company of Georgia. George and his father would take the streetcar to Five Points, which was a far different place at the turn of the century than it is today. There were street car tracks everywhere, trolley wires overhead, and still a good number of horses and wagons in the streets.[28] During the late 1880s and early 1890s, a large artesian well had crowded the open space at Five Points, but the water was condemned and the structure removed in 1893, two years before George Woodruff's birth. Even after the well's removal, however, the area remained a gathering place for businessmen and downtown visitors, and its brief presence had left its mark on building and traffic patterns at Five Points. Street car tracks were laid by the Consolidated and other companies during the few years the structure was standing, and they had to be routed *around* the well, a necessity that resulted in an open space that for many years held a flag pole and even today remains a clearing that expands gradually into Woodruff Park.[29]

At the time George Woodruff started visiting the Trust Company with his father, the bank had its small office behind the elevators on the first floor of the old Equitable Building, which stood on the northeast corner of Edgewood Avenue and Park Place where the Trust

George W. Woodruff in about 1905, at approximately age ten.

(Credit: Lenney-Atlanta)

Company Banking Annex is now located. Completed in 1891 by Joel Hurt's East Atlanta Land Company, the Equitable Building was underwritten by the Equitable Life Assurance Society, a New York firm, from which the building took its name. At the time it was built, the eight-story Equitable Building enjoyed the dual distinction of being both the highest and the first steel structure in the Southeast.[30]

The Trust Company of Georgia had its beginnings as the Commercial Travelers Savings Bank, founded in 1891 by a group of investors including Joel Hurt. In 1892, Hurt read a paper before the fledgling institution's directors urging that the little savings bank change its course and become a large trust company with a paid-in capital of not less than $250,000. In the fall of 1893, the directors of the Commercial Travelers Savings Bank, who by then included Ernest Woodruff, took action on Hurt's suggestion. The institution was renamed Trust Company of Georgia and was licensed to manage trusts and engage in investment banking and the underwriting of securities.[31]

Artesian well at Five Points, taken in 1892 looking down Edgewood Avenue. Drilling for the well began in 1884, but the water was condemned and the structure removed in November of 1893. The block immediately behind the well was purchased by the Ernest and Emily Woodruff foundation in 1971 at the instigation of George and Robert Woodruff for $10,000,000. The block was cleared to make way for Central City Park, renamed Woodruff Park in 1985. Notice the old Trust Company Building, then the Equitable Building, under construction immediately to the left of the first utility pole visible on the right side of the picture.

(Courtesy of the Atlanta Historical Society)

At George Woodruff's earliest memory of the Trust Company, there were only three employees—John Wheat was secretary and treasurer, Harry Steel was the bank's stenographer, and Ernest Woodruff had been named president in 1904 after an eleven-year stint on the board of directors.[32] Woodruff labored tirelessly for the Trust Company's success, and his sons grew up with a profound respect and loyalty to the institution. George especially took to heart his father's early lessons in frugality. "Save whatever money you can," his father would tell him. "Don't spend all the money you've got."[33] Very soon after Ernest became involved with the bank, he brought home passbooks for the savings accounts he had opened for each of his sons with one dollar each, and the boys were expected to add whatever they could to the original amount. "Be conservative," Ernest Woodruff frequently admonished, and his son George was, avoiding throughout his life the ostentatious lifestyle of many people of similar wealth.

Emily Winship Woodruff, with son George on left and son Henry on right, taken around 1908. The photograph is an interesting period piece, as well as an apt characterization of Woodruff family life. The family traveled a good deal, both together and individually, and had an inordinate fondness for automobiles.

George would ride down Edgewood Avenue with him to the Trust Company, gladly accepting the penalty of walking or taking the streetcar back home. People who heard the car coming would leave what they were doing to watch its progress, and when it stopped, bystanders would come up to touch it and sometimes ask for rides. On Sundays after church, the whole family would get into the Oldsmobile and, attracting a great deal of attention along the route, drive to Hapeville, Buckhead, College Park, Lithia Springs, or Marietta, taking care not to startle horses on the way. Sometimes they would stop by the side of the road for a picnic, and other times they would simply enjoy the scenery and the ride. Motor traffic was extremely light for the first five or six years after the Woodruffs got the car, and no license was required to drive on the roads. After a time, however, more and more people began buying cars, and gradually, even the mules and wagons used for delivery purposes were replaced by trucks. While Emily Woodruff was not quite adventuresome enough to drive the car alone, she refused to let progress pass her by. Shortly after the Oldsmobile's arrival at 708 Edgewood Avenue, Emily acquired a little electric car, controlled by a single lever and sized and built like a small carriage. Happily mobile, Mrs. Woodruff drove herself all over town on her various errands.[42]

While the Woodruffs did travel a good deal in Atlanta, on at least one occasion, they ventured forth to far more distant horizons than Stone Mountain or Lithonia. In 1908, deciding that they needed a vacation, Ernest Woodruff arranged to borrow the luxury Pullman car owned by Charles A. Wickersham, president of the Atlanta & West Point Railroad. He purchased the twenty tickets required to have the car included in various trains along the chosen route, packed Robert, George, Henry, Emily, Frances and George Walters (Emily's youngest sister and her husband), and a nephew from Columbus into the Pullman and headed across the country on a two-month trip.[43]

Staying in the Pullman pulled off on a side track, the party stopped all the way along their route to see various cities and other points of interest. The car was equipped with staterooms, berths, an observation platform, a kitchen, and a dining room, allowing the Woodruffs to eat in the Pullman car aside from meals in hotels during side trips. Traveling to Mexico City, Salt Lake City, Los Angeles, San Francisco, Seattle, and Chicago, the family visited parks, beaches, zoos, noted buildings, and monuments, enjoying particularly San Francisco's steep hills and street cars. The high point of the trip, George Woodruff remembered more than seventy-five years later, was the tour through Yellowstone National Park, a week long drive in a stage coach pulled by six horses. Trains and automobiles were not allowed in the park, so the Woodruff party left the Pullman car outside the West Yellowstone gate and proceeded through by dirt roads, with a professional driver to guide the stage coach along the way, the family the horses. Staying at hotels in the park along the way, the family could only travel about fifteen miles a day because of the rough condition of the roads, and when it rained, the stage coach would quickly become mired in the mud. These inconveniences, however, seemed minor in comparison to the natural grandeur of the deep valleys, eroded lava flows, obsidian cliffs, paint pots, hot rivers, and geysers. The tour of Yellowstone was capped off by a night at the lodge at Old Faithful, and George Woodruff never forgot the sight of the nation's most famous geyser erupting. The family returned to the Pullman after about seven days in the park and continued their winding route back to Atlanta.[44]

In 1910, around two years after the Woodruffs' grand western tour, George Woodruff finished his eight years at the Edgewood Avenue School and began high school at Tech High on Marietta Street, about a mile past Five Points. On days when it was clear and warm, Woodruff would ride his bicycle from Inman Park to school, returning home for lunch. When it rained, he would take the street car, and although he was probably safer than he would have been on his bicycle in the rain, he still arrived at school soaked to the skin from the mile walk from the end of the streetcar line at Five Points. Woodruff very much enjoyed Tech High, as he was finally able to develop his mechanical and technological interests in an academic setting. Before he had spent more than a year at the school, he realized that he would want to go to Georgia Tech for his college studies, so he applied himself with particular energy to his classes in machine shop and mechanical drawing.[45]

During George Woodruff's last few years at Edgewood Avenue School and first year at Tech High, the Woodruff family went through several adjustments and changes. In 1908, eldest brother Robert, known to George and Henry as "Buddie," finished at Georgia Military Academy, later renamed Woodward Academy. He went off to Emory College in Oxford, Georgia, where it was then located, but while Robert was phenomenally talented in a variety of fields, traditional academics was not one of them. After a little more than five months at the school, eager to get his start in business, Robert

George W. and Robert W. Woodruff on the tennis court in about 1908. George would have been about thirteen and Robert nineteen at the time.

moved back home, went on the trip out West with his family, and started work in February of 1909 at the General Pipe and Foundry Company for sixty cents a day, less than half of his allowance while he was a student at Emory.[46]

Around the time of Robert's return home to Edgewood Avenue, grandfather George Waldo Woodruff began coming up from Columbus for extended periods to stay with the family. His wife, Virginia Lindsay Woodruff, had been in poor health for several years and had been living with their daughter and son-in-law, Annie Bright and Joel Hurt, in their Inman Park home. Grampa Woodruff, as Robert, George, and Henry called him, would come to Atlanta to be near his wife and to visit with each of his children and both sets of grandchildren, but he would stay primarily with the Woodruff family, as the Hurt household had also expanded to take in Joel's mother, Lucy Apperson Hurt.[47] The Woodruff sons were fond of their grandfather, and George remembers him sitting in his chair in the library or the receiving room with his ever-present ear trumpet, a constant companion from the time his deafness first became apparent at the age of twenty-three. The elder George Woodruff was interested in his surroundings and his grandchildren, but never interfered with their activities, friends, or schedules. The family would communicate with him by shouting into the trumpet, and George Woodruff, who like his grandfather, father, and brother was quite hard of hearing in his later years, said of him humorously, "my grandfather was the only person I ever knew who was deafer than I am."[48]

On January 23, 1911, after a gradual decline, Virginia Lindsay Woodruff died at the home of her daughter Annie Bright, where she had spent the last several years of her life. Obituaries in both Columbus and Atlanta papers noted her longtime devotion to charity and good works, particularly in the service of injured Confederate soldiers during the Civil War. Her whole Atlanta family accompanied her body to Columbus for burial.[49] George Waldo Woodruff continued to return to Atlanta periodically to stay with the Woodruff family, but on one of his trips back to Columbus to look after his business interests, he died suddenly, probably of a heart attack, on November 4, 1911, at the home of his eldest son, Henry. He was eighty-six.

George W. Woodruff, who had arrived in Columbus from Southington, Connecticut, in 1842 at the age of eighteen, was mourned in his adopted city as one of its oldest and most prominent citizens. Despite his northern roots and family remaining in Connecticut, Woodruff had believed so much in the strength of the Southern position that he actively supported the war effort and even kept his wealth in confederate currency during the Civil War, a conflict which for him in particular held the often repeated possibility of "brother fighting brother." After emerging from the war virtually penniless, Woodruff went on through persistence and ingenuity to rebuild his business and investments, ultimately amassing another fortune and dying a millionaire—"one of the wealthiest citizens of Columbus." Along with a monetary inheritance, George Woodruff's heirs were left with the equally valuable legacies of many generations of business sense and civic responsibility. As one historian wrote, "George Waldo Woodruff instilled in his children and grandchildren his belief that successful citizens have an obligation to work toward the success of their community."[50]

In 1913, just before his eighteenth birthday, the elder George W. Woodruff's namesake entered the freshman class of Georgia School of Technology to study mechanical engineering, following both of his grandfathers into a career of industry and manufacturing.[51] While George Woodruff was interested in his father's focus on capitalism and large scale investment, he was far more fascinated by the actual operations of business, especially in the technical and mechanical areas. His enrollment at Georgia Tech represented a continuation of the interests he had developed at Tech High, and although the curriculum and schedule were rigorous, Woodruff's commitment to his chosen course of study overcame at least a good portion of any natural frustration at the long hours and difficult material.

While he attended Georgia Tech, Woodruff lived at home in Inman Park, commuting between his house and school by means of his newly acquired motorcycle, a bright red Indian of which he was very proud. The motorcycle ran on two cylinders and had a small seat behind the driver's seat where Woodruff would sometimes carry friends less fortunate in their means of transportation. The cobblestone roads were rough and full of ruts, and although helmets were neither required nor worn, Woodruff managed to avoid accidents and injuries.[52]

Kenneth Gordon Matheson, a man Woodruff greatly admired, was the president of Tech when he enrolled in 1913, and the university was in a period of growth in both the curriculum and the physical plant. Woodruff studied algebra, geometry, trigonometry, and calculus under Dr. Richard H. Lowndes, and English, Spanish, and other basic liberal arts courses under a variety of different professors. Classes started at eight o'clock each morning, broke at twelve for lunch, and resumed at one o'clock for wood shop, machine shop, me-

*George W. Woodruff in about 1915, while attending Georgia Tech in Atlanta. George Woodruff met Irene King, his future wife, in 1915, telling her on their first meeting that he would marry her one day.
Note the stiff collar.*

chanical drawing, and other technical application classes until five.[53] Preparation for academic classes each day was demanding, and Woodruff's notebooks from Tech contain ample evidence of diligent outside work and studied precision in problem solving.[54]

Although Tech's physical plant was far less developed in 1913 than it is today, the facilities were still impressive. The campus boasted Carnegie Library, an administration building, several shops, the Joseph Brown Whitehead Hospital, the A. French Textile Building, the electrical building, Lyman Hall Chemistry Lab, the Georgia Tech Y.M.C.A., the foundry, and several dormitories.[55] Grant Field, however, was just that—a bare athletic field with no stands or other facilities. The students called the field Tech Flats, and they would drive up to the sidelines to watch athletic events, with the cars themselves serving as bleachers.[56] Although Woodruff was not himself involved in college athletics, he was a loyal supporter of the football team, and he would often fill his father's seven-passenger Stephens-Duryea or Peerless with his Kappa Alpha fraternity brothers and their dates to cheer on the football team at Tech Flats. After the game, the party would go on to a dance hall or to dinner at the Piedmont Driving Club or the Capital City Club, always, despite their youth and enthusiasm, a mannerly and restrained group of young men. Their meetings were very solemn, Woodruff later said, and "there was very little hell-raising or drinking."[57]

Kappa Alpha Fraternity

ALPHA SIGMA CHAPTER

Founded 1865 *Established 1898*

FRATRES IN FACULTATE

Dr. K. G. Matheson   Prof. W. G. Perry   Prof. H. Hughes   Prof. W. S. Nelms

1914

W. E. Dunwody, Jr.   M. Pound   J. M. Reifsneider

1915

C. B. Grimes   H. L. Herrington   K. P. Ribble
W. M. Robinson   W. P. Sloan   B. D. Smith
P. Sneed   W. A. Troy   J. W. Turner

1916

R. Battle   R. S. Fleet   R. H. McNulty   R. E. Lester

1917

C. A. Brooks   T. Coleman   J. S. Disosway
G. Eastman   W. Moore   A. Redding
A. H. Weems   G. W. Woodruff   V. Wooley

1918

M. L. Brittian, Jr.   L. Willett

Kappa Alpha fraternity roster and picture from Georgia Tech's yearbook, the Blue Print, in 1914. George Woodruff is the first on the left in the third row. (From Georgia Tech Blue Print, Institute Archives, Price Gilbert Memorial Library, Georgia Institute of Technology.)

Another popular social event for young people when Woodruff was in college was the house party, usually a weekend-long affair where a chaperoned group would visit, play games, and generally socialize with one another. It was at such a house party given at the West Peachtree Street home of Woodruff's maternal aunt, Maria Elizabeth Winship Bates, known to the Woodruff brothers as Aunt Lizzie, that George W. Woodruff was to meet his future wife. During his second year at Tech, Woodruff had been dating a young woman named Sarah Eubanks fairly regularly when, at his Aunt Lizzie's 1915 house party, his lady friend introduced him to her good friend, Irene King. Totally charmed, Woodruff announced to his new acquaintance that he intended to marry her some day. While the seventeen-year-old Irene laughed at this bold assertion and Woodruff later claims, "I was just talking," he nevertheless immediately terminated his relationship with Sarah Eubanks in favor of Miss King, beginning a three year courtship and a lifelong love.

ENDNOTES

¹Jack Johnson Spalding, "Piedmont Park," *The Atlanta Historical Bulletin,* 2:11 (1973): 6.

²Franklin M. Garrett, *Atlanta and Its Environs: A Chronicle of Its People and Events,* 2 vols. (Athens, Georgia: University of Georgia Press, 1969) 2:313.

³Ibid., 2:329.

⁴Personal interview with George W. Woodruff, 31 December 1985.

⁵Personal interviews with George W. Woodruff, 25 October 1985 and 20 May 1986.

⁶Ibid.

⁷Personal interviews with George W. Woodruff, 25 October 1985 and 11 September 1986.

⁸Personal interview with George W. Woodruff, 20 May 1986.

⁹Personal interview with George W. Woodruff, 25 October 1985. See *The Atlanta Journal,* "Robt. Winship is Paralyzed," 28 August 1899.

¹⁰Personal interviews with George W. Woodruff, 25 October 1985 and 20 May 1986.

¹¹From a newspaper clipping "Beautiful Home of Mr. and Mrs. Woodruff" in Emily Winship Woodruff's family scrapbook, n.d., n.p. It is currently in the possession of Jane Woodruff.

The Atlanta Journal, "Beautiful New Home in Inman Park Being Built for Mr. Ernest Woodruff," 26 August 1899.

¹²"Beautiful Home of Mr. and Mrs. Woodruff," n.p.

Personal interview with George W. Woodruff, 25 October 1985.

¹³"Beautiful Home of Mr. and Mrs. Woodruff," n.p.

¹⁴Personal interview with George W. Woodruff, 25 October 1985.

¹⁵Ibid.

¹⁶Edge, *Joel Hurt,* 106.

¹⁷Personal interview with George W. Woodruff, 25 October 1985.

¹⁸Edge, *Joel Hurt,* 106, quoting an 1891 magazine article found in Joel Hurt's scrapbook, "Like a Romance, but a Fait Accompli, Brilliant in Con-

ception, Perfect in Execution. Inman Park, the Now Famous Suburb of the Most Famous Southern City," n.d., n.p.

[19]Ibid, 257. Also see George W. Woodruff obituary.

[20]Edge, *Joel Hurt,* 104.

[21]Personal interview with William King Meadow, 22 July 1983.

[22]Edge, *Joel Hurt,* 194, 197.

[23]Ibid., 215.

[24]Garrett, *Atlanta and Its Environs,* 2:427.

[25]Ibid., 425.

When the line was built, all street car service ended at Fourteenth Street, and there were no cross streets or houses beyond that point. See Hughes Spalding, *The Spalding Family of Maryland, Kentucky, and Georgia from 1658 to 1965* 2 vols. (Atlanta: The Stein Printing Co., 1965) 2:125.

[26]Edge, *Joel Hurt,* 209.

[27]Personal interview with George W. Woodruff, 25 October 1985.

[28]Personal interview with George W. Woodruff, 25 October 1985.

[29]Garrett, *Atlanta and Its Environs,* 2:77-78, 821. See Spalding, *The Spalding Family,* 2:125.

[30]Harold Martin, *Three Strong Pillars,* (Atlanta, n.p., 1973) 20.

[31]Ibid., 20.

[32]Personal interview with George W. Woodruff, 20 May 1986.

[33]Ibid.

[34]Ibid. Also see Coleman and Gurr, eds., *Georgia Biography,* 2:1083-1085.

[35]Personal interview with George W. Woodruff, 31 December 1985.

[36]Coleman and Gurr, eds., *Georgia Biography,* 2:1083-1085. See also Garrett, *Atlanta and Its Environs,* 2:413.

[37]Personal interview with George W. Woodruff, 20 May 1986.

[38]Coleman and Gurr, eds., *Georgia Biography,* 2:1083-1085.

[39]Personal interview with George W. Woodruff, 31 December 1985.

[40]Personal interview with James P. Williams, 6 September 1986.

[41]Personal interview with George W. Woodruff, 25 October 1985.

[42]Ibid.

Personal interview with George W. Woodruff, 11 September 1986.

[43]Personal interview with George W. Woodruff, 25 October 1985.

Charles Elliott, *"Mr. Anonymous": Robert W. Woodruff of Coca-Cola* (Atlanta: Cherokee Publishing Company, 1982) 89.

[44]Personal interview with George W. Woodruff, 25 October 1985.

[45]Personal interviews with George W. Woodruff, 25 October 1985 and 7 October 1986.

[46]Elliott, "Mr. Anonymous," 89.

[47]Edge, *Joel Hurt,* 115.

[48]Personal interview with George W. Woodruff, 20 May 1986.

[49]*The Atlanta Constitution,* "Mrs. G. W. Woodruff Called to Beyond," 24 January 1911 and *The Atlanta Journal,* "Mrs. Virginia Woodruff is Called To Rest," 24 January 1911.

[50] George W. Woodruff obituary. See also Margaret Laney Whitehead and Barbra Bogart, *City of Progress: A History of Columbus, Georgia 1828-1978* (Columbus, Georgia: The Columbus Office Supply Co., 1978) 568.

[51] Georgia School of Technology was renamed Georgia Institute of Technology in 1948 (Anne Bartlow, Institute Archives, Price Gilbert Memorial Library, Georgia Institute of Technology).

[52] Personal interview with George W. Woodruff, 3 January 1986.

[53] Personal interview with George W. Woodruff, 3 January 1986. See also Robert C. McMath, et al., *Engineering the New South: Georgia Tech 1885-1985,* (Athens, Georgia: University of Georgia Press, 1985) 107.

[54] George W. Woodruff's college notebooks are in the possession of his daughter, Jane Woodruff.

[55] Georgia School of Technology Announcements, 1912-1915, Institute Archives, Price Gilbert Memorial Library, Georgia Institute of Technology, 158.

[56] Personal interview with George W. Woodruff, 3 January 1986. The stands and facilities making up present day Grant Field were made possible through a donation from Atlanta capitalist John Grant, developer of the Grant Building in downtown Atlanta. (Personal interview with George W. Woodruff, 3 January 1986.)

[57] Personal interview with George W. Woodruff, 3 January 1986.

Chapter Three

An Epistolary Romance

George Woodruff's and Irene King's romance blossomed during the 1914-15 school year as the pair attended dinner parties, theater parties, dances in dance halls, movies, and ballgames. George, still driving his motorcycle back and forth from Tech, would also often squeeze in additional time with Irene in the late afternoons, visiting her after class and staying until around dinner time. Irene later reminisced that she could hear Georgia Tech's five o'clock whistle blow way over on North Avenue and then, just as predictably and only minutes later, the sound of George's red Indian as it puttered up Ponce de Leon Avenue to the King family home.[1] Although the motorcycle had an extra seat on the back for passengers and George often transported his brothers and friends that way, Irene was strictly forbidden to ride on the motorcycle, and George would borrow the family car to take her out. The one time that curiosity got the better of her, Clyde King, who referred to the Indian as "that horrid thing," discovered the breach of rules and restricted her social life for a time in an effort to help her resist future temptation. King reinforced the lesson with frequent reports to his daughter that he had once again seen George driving his motorcycle "like a shot out of a gun."[2]

Irene Tift King was born in Atlanta on April 16, 1898, the first of Clyde and Clara Belle King's four children. Irene's father, Clyde Lanier King, was the son of the Reverend James Lawrence and Martha Anderson King and was born in 1875 in Lawrenceville, Georgia. In 1885, at the age of ten, he moved with his parents to Atlanta, where his father was to become the pastor of the Rock Spring Presbyterian Church. When he turned fifteen, Clyde King took his first job as a clerk with King Hardware Company, operated by George King, one of his older brothers. After doing general work in the store for several years, Clyde became the King Hardware Company's secretary and treasurer and continued in that capacity until some time after his marriage to Clara Belle Rushton on June 2, 1894.[3]

Clara Belle Rushton, the first of Robert E. and Ella Byron Wight Rushton's seven children, was born in Atlanta in 1877. Her mother,

Georgia Tech campus circa 1914, reproduced from Tech's yearbook, The Blue Print. George W. Woodruff attended Georgia Tech from the fall of 1913 through the spring of 1916 and remained loyal to the school all his life. (From the Georgia Tech Blue Print, Institute Archives, Price Gilbert Memorial Library, Georgia Institute of Technology.)

Ella Wight Rushton (1853-1926), Irene Tift King Woodruff's maternal grandmother.

(Credit: Smith & Motes-Atlanta)

Ella Rushton, was born in 1853 in Wightsville, Georgia, and graduated from Wesleyan Female College in 1873. In 1876, she married Robert Ellwood Rushton, who was born in Atlanta in 1849. The newlyweds moved into Rushton's father's home on Capitol Avenue, and Robert then began work with the Winship Machine Company, ultimately attaining the office of secretary when Robert and George Winship, George Woodruff's grandfather and great-uncle, decided to incorporate the company in 1878.[4] Clara Belle Rushton also was close to the Winship family, having become fast friends with Mary Frances Winship, Emily Winship Woodruff's younger sister, while attending Agnes Scott College. Clara Belle and "Mary Frank" belonged to a group of young women who called themselves "The Seven Mystic Maids" and remained close throughout their lives, documenting their friendship with a series of group photographs taken over a period of more than twenty-five years.[5]

Soon after their 1894 wedding, Clyde and Clara Belle King moved to a large two-story brick house at 274 Ponce de Leon Avenue, renumbered 430 in 1926, where their first child, Irene, was born in 1898. In 1902, Clyde King, then secretary and treasurer of his brother's hardware company, decided to go into business on his own. He

Clyde Lanier King and Clara Belle Rushton King, June 1897.

He found two partners, F. S. Dean and J. E. Powell, gathered $10,000 in capital, hired ten plant workers and five office and sales employees, and organized the Atlanta Agricultural Works, a company specializing in the manufacture of repair parts for plows.

The new company filled a manufacturing void in the largely agrarian South and became successful soon after its establishment. In its first year of operation, the Atlanta Agricultural Works grossed $25,000, and as earnings increased steadily thereafter, the firm quickly expanded into the production of many different types of farm equipment. The purchase of the patent for the Terrell Scrape, a widely used implement in the southeastern region at the time, was a

Irene King Woodruff's parents, Mr. and Mrs. Clyde L. King, lived in this house at 274 Ponce de Leon Avenue, renumbered 430 in 1926, prior to completing their house at 1010 (later renumbered 1386) Ponce de Leon Avenue in 1911.

tremendously beneficial influence on sales, and the company soon embarked on a wide-scale program of expansion, acquiring several competing plants in the area and merging them into its operation under the name of the Atlanta Plow Company in 1920. The firm eventually became one of the leading manufacturers of farm implements in the South and maintained a successful export trade, particularly with South American countries. In 1932, when Clyde King retired from the company and his son, Clyde L. King, Jr., took his place as president, the firm was renamed King Plow.[6]

In 1902, the year of the Atlanta Agricultural Works' formation, a second child, Clyde King, Jr., was born to Clyde and Clara Belle King. A daughter, Clara Belle, followed in 1906, and the family, growing in number and prosperity, began plans for a new home. They chose to build in Druid Hills, another residential area that Joel Hurt had begun developing, this time with the design help of the famed landscape architect Frederick Law Olmsted, creator of New York's Central Park and the gardens at Biltmore, the Vanderbilts' estate. Olmsted and Hurt, who was also trained as a landscape architect, designed the Druid Hills portion of Ponce de Leon as a beautifully landscaped boulevard, with Deepdene, Dellwood, Oak Grove, Virgile, and Springdale parks laid out parallel to the roadway from east to west and a streetcar line running down the middle.[7]

Druid Hills became an extremely popular area to build as soon as lots were available for sale, and Clyde King was one of the first buyers, purchasing a lot on the northwest corner of Ponce de Leon Avenue and Oakdale Road for $9,000 in February of 1910. Construction began immediately on the large brick structure, which was the second home to be built in the Druid Hills area.[8] Such prestigious Atlantans as the founders of the Georgia Power Company and the Retail Credit Company, along with various family members and business associates of early Coca-Cola Company owner Asa G. Candler, followed suit, hiring Philip Shutze, Neel Reid, and other well-known architects to design their large and luxurious homes. Architect Walter T. Downing, who designed the Woodruffs' house on Edgewood Avenue, also built a home in the area, and by the 1920s, the Druid Hills section of Ponce de Leon Avenue had been called "*the* street in Atlanta," second only to Inman Park in its roster of prominent local citizens.[9]

The Kings' new home was completed in 1911, and the family moved from their 274 Ponce de Leon address, which fell near Charles Allen Drive, out to the heart of Druid Hills, 1010 Ponce de Leon Avenue, renumbered 1386 in 1926.[10] In 1914, three years after the move, the Kings' last child, son John, was born in the new home. It was also in the house at 1010 Ponce de Leon that George Woodruff and Irene King did most of their courting, sitting alone on the porch on summer evenings and in the den inside during cooler weather.[11]

At the time that George and Irene met, George was not yet twenty, Irene had just turned seventeen, and both sets of parents considered them far too young to date each other exclusively. Both the

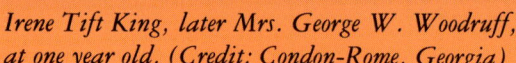

Irene Tift King at age three.

Irene Tift King, later Mrs. George W. Woodruff, at one year old. (Credit: Condon-Rome, Georgia)

Irene Tift King at approximately age ten.

Irene Tift King at approximately age twelve.

The home of Irene King Woodruff's parents, Mrs. and Mrs. Clyde L. King, at 1010 (later renumbered 1386) Ponce de Leon Avenue. The lot, located on the northwestern corner of Oakdale Road and Ponce de Leon Avenue, was bought by the Kings on February 10, 1915, from the Druid Hills Company for $9,000. The home was completed in 1911, and the King family moved from their previous home at 274 Ponce de Leon Avenue. Mr. and Mrs. King spent the rest of their lives in this home, and their two daughters, Irene King Woodruff and Clara Belle King Bivings, were married there.

Woodruffs and the Kings strongly encouraged their offspring to attend social events with a variety of different companions, but the Kings found Irene unenthusiastic at their suggestions, and the Woodruffs had only minimal success with George. The two sought other company only when they were unavoidably separated, but these infrequent "infidelities" nonetheless provided fertile ground for the two to test each other's affection and develop new levels of commitment. Even at the age of ninety-one, George Woodruff easily recalled seventy-year-old jealousy: "She would always tell me when she had dates with other boys," he said on one occasion. "It just made me crazy."[12]

One of Woodruff's Kappa Alpha fraternity brothers was a particularly tenacious rival for Irene's time and affection, and she would strategically introduce his name as often as she dared. When Irene and George were separated by family vacations or one of the two was away at school, flurries of correspondence would be exchanged over this interloper's frequent "affronts," which ranged from asking her for dates too often to trying to sit with her at church or visiting her at her family's home. To pique George's interest, Irene once concluded significantly in a postscript, "I have something to tell you in tomorrow's letter about Jay Bird."[13] True to her word and after letting George worry for a day, she reported in her next letter, "Yesterday a package came for me . . . It was a great big picture of Jay Bird. What on earth must I do about it?"[14] George's response was swift and sure. "Destroy it immediately," he wrote, "preferably by fire. . . . I suppose Jay Bird thought that the time was ripe to start over again, owing to the fact the competition was fifteen hundred miles away."[15] Having received the desired response affirming his devotion to her, Irene complied with George's direction and wrote back, "I don't care what he thinks of me. I don't love him and I never will."[16] With the bold Jay Bird then at least temporarily at bay, another Lothario would burst onto the scene. "Dearest," Irene began in telling George of her latest admirer, "I am writing this with the silver pencil Lewis Ledsinger gave me yesterday afternoon."[17]

George too looked for reassurance of Irene's affection, keeping her apprised when he met a young lady at school or while traveling with his family. "She was the cutest, prettiest little girl I ever saw," George wrote of a casual acquaintance in 1916, and that was enough to send Irene into a teasing frenzy of concern.[18] "Who was the little girl that you were so struck with? Now that you have met the *cutest, prettiest* little girl you ever saw, and can write to her, I guess you don't want to hear from me so often . . . I guess I'll be forgotten entirely, and nobody will care if I never come home."[19] George of course immediately assured her that such a state of affairs could never come to pass, and the two continued their daily and loving correspondence.

After spending a great deal of time together over the spring and summer of 1915, George and Irene were suddenly separated as Irene started school that fall at National Park Seminary in Forest Glen, Maryland, and George continued living at home and commuting to Tech on his red Indian motorcycle. While the two were clearly and vocally unhappy about the distance between them, their separation did afford them ample opportunities to meet and socialize with a variety of people. That they continued to write to each other daily and, at ages seventeen and twenty, stayed fast in their loyalty to each other is a testament to the depth of a commitment that endured and thrived for sixty-seven years. Throughout the periods when they were apart, their long letters were vehicles for sharing their daily activities, friends, triumphs, and concerns. "Just imagine you had a date with me," Irene wrote on one occasion. "Sit down and write me a long, long letter answering all my questions and telling me everything else you know, nice things and troubles too."[20]

Irene chose National Park Seminary from a small group of women's junior colleges, mostly in the Washington, D.C. area, that she visited with her parents over a period of several weeks during the summer of 1915.[21] National Park stood out for its faculty and its beautiful buildings and grounds, and Irene maintained her high opinion of those two attributes despite periodic disenchantment with what she perceived as slavish scheduling and a seemingly endless pro-

> **National Park Seminary**
> Forest Glen, Md.
>
> Feb. 20, 1916.
>
> Dear George,—
>
> I received your letter to-day and so glad to get it, because Sunday is such a lonely day here, and that is the only thing that would help matters a bit. And it certainly does. Your letter to-day was doubly appreciated because I didn't get one from

fusion of rules.[22] Her letters during her years at National Park were almost invariably in pencil and practically illegible, as correspondence was disfavored by the housemothers and teachers, and Irene had to be prepared at any moment to feign class preparation should one of the several stern and unyielding housemothers burst into her room. Pencil was required for both notes and homework assignments, and, Irene claimed in her letters, even the sharpest-eyed study monitors found pencilled letters and reading notes indistinguishable.[23]

Although Irene did find the schedule somewhat taxing and the sheer number of rules vexing, she very much enjoyed her course of

Nineteen sixteen postcard from National Park Seminary in Forest Glen, Maryland, where Irene attended from 1915 to 1917.

study, which included science, English, music and voice lessons, housewifery, home nursing, home cooking, plain sewing, and dressmaking.[24] She was a diligent student, an active sorority member, and an enthusiastic participant in many extracurricular activities. Ernest Woodruff, who regularly called her at school when he passed through Washington on business, reported to his son that he could tell from the sound of her voice how pleased she was with school and how happy she seemed to be. Although she had been ill and underweight during the summer before she started school, she thrived at National Park and soon boasted that she had gained ten pounds since the year began. Unable to resist such an opening, George responded quickly, "Well, Fatty, I hope you are not worrying on that account—little fat girls are so cute."[25]

After Irene left Atlanta for National Park, George continued to do well at Georgia Tech and to participate in his fraternity's activities, but he missed Irene badly and was unenthusiastic about attending functions without her. He would take another date to K. A. parties and dances, but he was always sure to send Irene an invitation for the event, along with whatever party favors the K. A.s had planned for the occasion.[26] He found some comfort in the company of his mother and his brother Robert's wife, Nell, who was living with the family on Edgewood Avenue while Robert was traveling extensively for the White Motor Company. George would proudly escort Emily and Nell to shows, parties, family gatherings, and church, always gallant enough to keep his silence about wishing Irene could

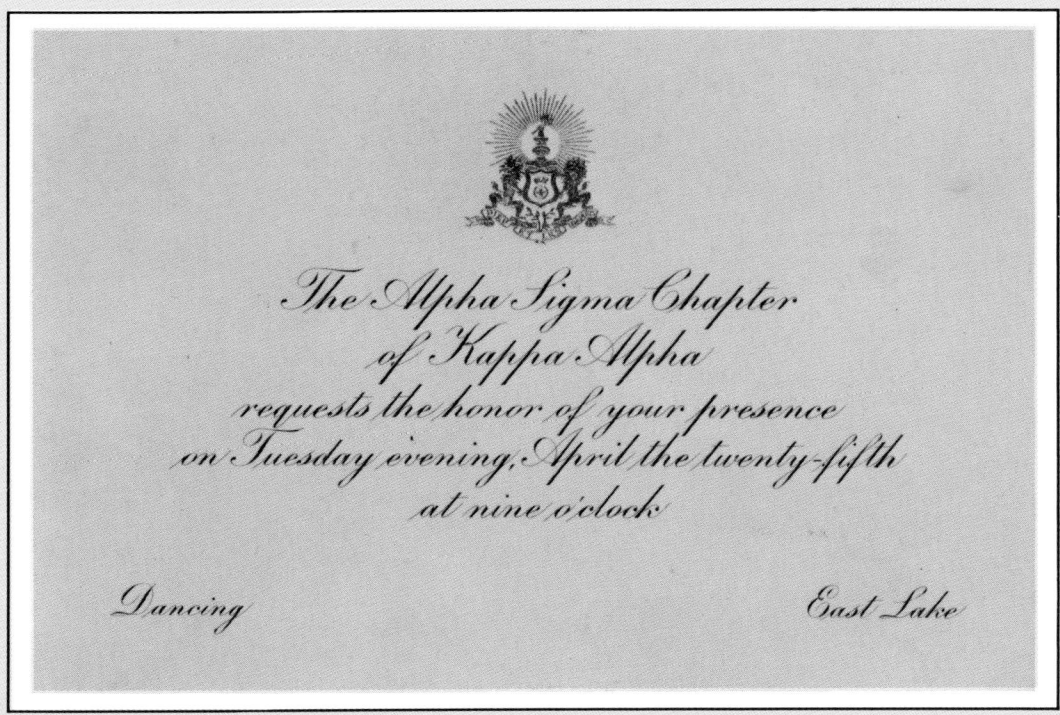

Invitation to a 1916 K.A. dance sent to Irene King at National Park Seminary in Forest Glen, Maryland. Woodruff was a K.A. at Georgia Tech and never failed to send Irene King invitations to and favors from all fraternity functions even when she was away at school.

take their places. After one such outing, George wrote to Irene, "If it were only you that I was taking around, I would be satisfied. But if it can't be you, Nell and Mama are the only ones it shall be."[27] Ever trying to assuage his melancholy, Emily and Nell even tried taking turns showing him *their* old love letters written to and by Ernest and Robert Woodruff, but George remained difficult to cheer.

George Woodruff completed his third year at Georgia Tech in 1916 at the age of twenty, excited about the year's academic accomplishments and looking forward to Irene's return home for summer break. George still very much enjoyed his study of mechanical engineering and was constantly applying his knowledge both in his summer jobs at the Atlantic Steel Company and the Atlantic Ice & Coal Company and in the context of his own keen interest in things mechanical. He loved machines of all kinds, particularly cars, and was enthusiastic in explaining the operation, maintenance, and repair of automobile engines to friends and family members who were new car owners. He worked on his own motorcycle and the family cars, and he liked nothing better than to attend an automobile show and engage the salesmen in lively discussion and defense of their products' engine mechanism and thermal efficiency.[28]

During June of 1916, the Woodruff family spent several weeks traveling by passenger steamer, train, and automobile in the Great

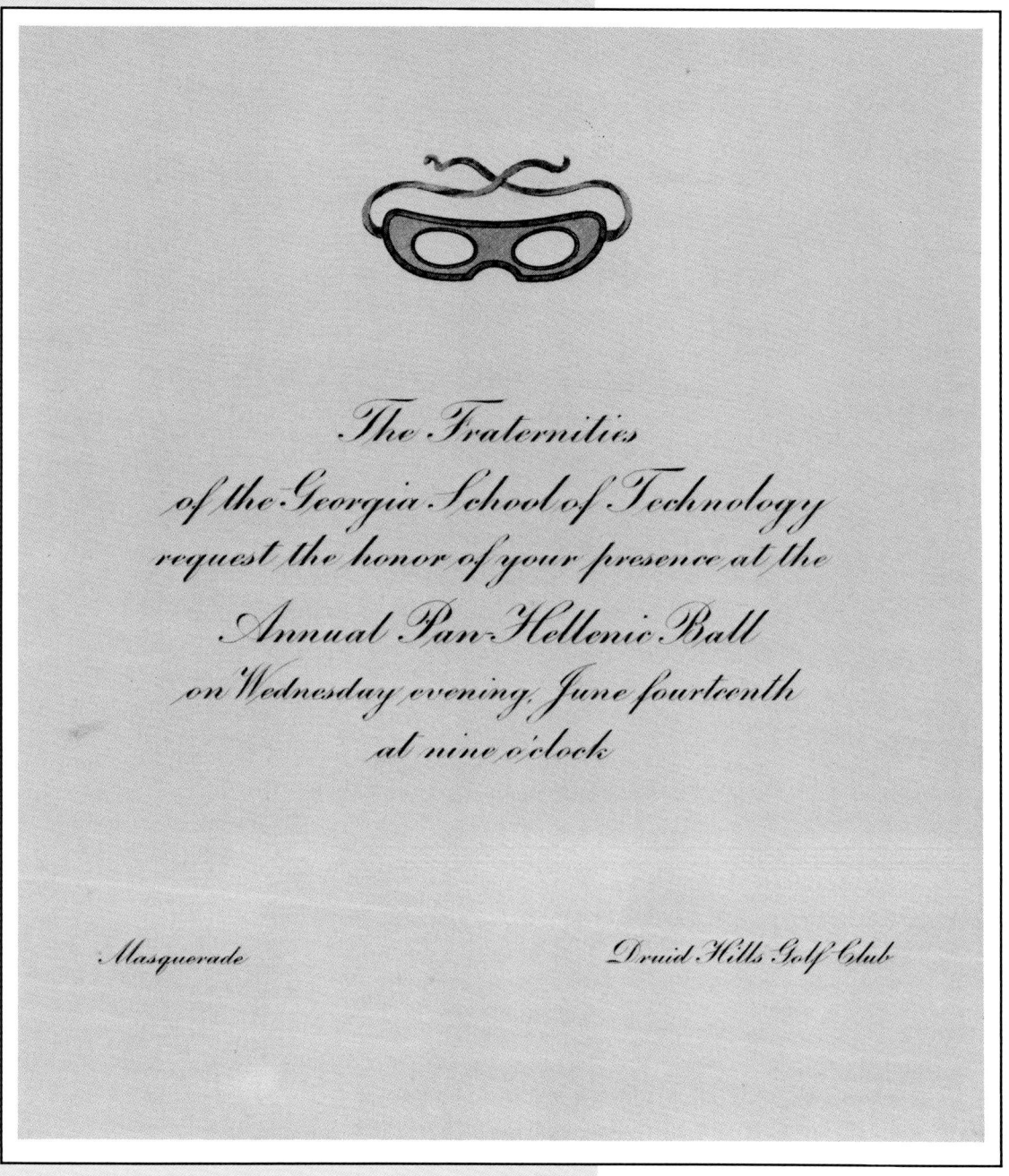

A 1916 invitation to a Georgia Tech Pan Hellenic Ball sent to Irene King at school in Maryland.

Lakes region, visiting Buffalo, Niagara Falls, Syracuse, Canandaigua, Saratoga Springs, and New York City, where George enjoyed making business calls with his father. He also wrote to Irene of dinner on the train with Samuel Candler Dobbs, who was Asa G. Candler's nephew and the vice president and general sales and advertising manager of The Coca-Cola Company. The family also had dinner at the Statler Hotel in New York City with Robert Woodruff's employer, Walter White, the owner of the White Motor Company.[29] George relished his time with Dobbs, White, and other businessmen on the trip, but he also wrote extensively about the road conditions in the Northeast and the many different makes of automobiles he saw while traveling. "I wish you could see the car we are going in," Woodruff wrote of the new White automobile the family would drive. "They finished building it today, and it is one of the prettiest I ever saw. . . . The country up here is wonderful, and every road is beautifully paved and as smooth as glass. It sometimes gets tiresome—there is such a sameness and never a bump."[30]

Perhaps the family's trip to the Northeast influenced his decision, or perhaps it was enduring a year in Atlanta with Irene in Maryland, but in any case, George Woodruff decided over the summer of 1916 not to return to Tech in the fall, and in late September, he began a tour of Northeastern schools in an attempt to find a university that would accept him for enrollment as a senior for the fall term. He first visited the Wharton School of Business at the University of Pennsylvania and then went on to Cornell University in Ithaca, New York, traveling via Owego to make the train connections.[31] "Ithaca is a very lively little town of sixteen thousand," Woodruff reported upon his arrival. "If I should decide to enter Cornell, from the looks of things, I should have anything but a dull time." Although he thought Cornell had a lively social atmosphere and a beautiful campus with "big, handsome buildings," Woodruff was less enthusiastic about the Finger Lakes region's topography and climate, writing to Irene, "Ithaca is down in a kind of valley, and the school is on top of a high hill. The hill is so steep, the street cars won't even stop on it, for they can't start again. It is particularly bad in wet weather, and it has been raining all day today." In the end, however, it was neither the backbreaking hills nor the unpleasant weather that resolved Woodruff's decision on Cornell. After meeting with the registrar, he found it would take him three years to graduate from the university, so he moved on to his next stop.[32]

From Ithaca, Woodruff returned to New Jersey, where he toured the campus at Princeton and spoke with the school's professors and registrar. While his prospects there at first looked hopeful, after several days the admissions committee told him that if he were to enter Princeton for the fall term, he would have to be classified as a sophomore. While Woodruff had amply satisfied the requirements for the junior class at Georgia Tech, the combination of different programs and more developed standards at the Northern schools stood in the way of his entrance at his own class level. Somewhat discouraged and very lonely, Woodruff wrote gloomily to Irene,

> I telegraphed Papa this morning and asked him about which I must do, enter as a sophomore at Princeton, or go to the Wharton School of Finance in the University of Pennsylvania. I suppose it will be tomorrow before I hear from him, which gives me another twenty-four hours of suspense. I'm almost disgusted with the whole business now. . . . I suppose you are at school by this time and as happy as a lark. . . . I wish I were [at school] or at least some place, so I'd know what I am going to do.[33]

While it was George Woodruff's own idea to leave Tech to attend a Northeastern school, it is undeniable that Ernest Woodruff took a strong interest in his son's choice of colleges. Education was important to the elder Woodruff, who had already fought and lost a higher education battle with George's elder brother, Robert. Robert, who did not enjoy high school, enjoyed college less and was intent on getting out of what he considered the sterile environment of academia and into business, where his real genius lay. Ernest disapproved vehemently and thundered at his son in complete frustration the now often-quoted words, "Damn it, Bob, it's three generations from shirtsleeves to shirtsleeves. Learn something."[34]

While Robert was unaffected by his father's loudly expressed preferences regarding his education and promptly left Emory University to start work at the General Pipe and Foundry Company, George was both more obliging and truly interested in his studies and their effect on his future. In his final decision concerning colleges, George was looking for his father's advice, but he had his own ideas about the kind of education he sought. After leaving Princeton, he traveled to Boston to look at Boston Tech, as most people then referred to the Massachusetts Institute of Technology, and found that although he would have to begin the fall term as a junior rather than a senior, the curriculum and facilities well justified the additional year required to graduate. "Boston Tech only has one building," George wrote enthusiastically to Irene, "but what a building it is. It even has its own power plant and telephone exchange."[35] He sent his father a telegram outlining his decision-making process on October 5th, and by the next week, George W. Woodruff had received Ernest's approval and had started full speed at Massachusetts Institute of Technology.

Finding living quarters in Boston proved difficult at first, and Woodruff spent the first few nights in town sharing a room at 434 Massachusetts Avenue with a former Georgia Tech student whom he had met by chance while crossing the Massachusetts Avenue Bridge from Cambridge into Boston. The two young men, uprooted from their friends and displaced from their native habitat, ate their meals at a nearby lunch counter and mused over the unfamiliarity of their surroundings. "*One* has to lift *one's* foot almost knee high every time *one* steps," George wrote to Irene, lampooning both the region's speech and weather. "That's the way these Yankees talk; doesn't it kill you?"[36] It was loneliness, however, far more than the alien environment that sank George's spirits during his first few weeks in Boston. He lived for his mail, particularly from Irene, and became distraught if it did not arrive on time. "[I]t has been four days since I've heard from you, and I'm almost crazy," he wrote in October. " . . . I don't see why [your letter] was delayed so long, but I guess it's just my luck, because I wanted it so bad. . . . If it weren't for your picture, I don't think I could manage at all, because I'm terribly lonesome. . . . The only thing I have to look forward to is being with you. That's what keeps me going, and I hope it always will."[37] A brief delay in receiving mail led him to imagine the worst possible explanation: "This is the second day now, and still no letter. What in the world is the matter? I hope and pray you haven't been hurt . . . if I don't receive a letter tomorrow, you may expect a telegram saying I'm on my way to Forest Glen or any where you happen to be."[38] The lost letter soon arrived, delayed by nothing more menacing than the vagaries of the U.S. Postal system, but the tables were quickly turned, and George had to rush to respond to Irene's worried inquiries over not hearing from him for several days. "There is no reason you shouldn't get a letter every day," he wrote. "[My roommate] teases me for writing so often. He says he doesn't see how anyone could think so much of *anybody*."[39]

MASSACHUSETTS
INSTITUTE OF TECHNOLOGY
CAMBRIDGE

Sunday Night

My Precious little Girl;—

I wonder what you've been doing all day today, it's been terribly lonesome for me, I went to church this morning, and worked all the afternoon, so tonight I think I'll take a couple of hours off and see a movie.

George W. Woodruff in about 1918. The other young man is not identified.

Before two weeks were over, Woodruff had found an acceptable room in a three-story brick boarding house at 263 Newbury Street in Boston. His roommate was Jim Ferrall, a fellow Boston Tech student he had met in class, and they shared a small room on the third floor of the house.[40] While Woodruff had fond memories of the room when reflecting on his days at Boston Tech, time and sentimentality may have played a role in blurring the house's inadequacies, as his letters from that period treat his accommodations far less generously than do his memories. Upon seeing the room on a visit to Boston soon after George began the fall term, Ernest Woodruff tersely pronounced the room a firetrap and began issuing his son rapid-fire instructions on what sort of rope to purchase and how to secure it to the window frame in order to be ready to lower himself to the street "at any minute" should an emergency arise.[41] George himself quickly lost patience with his living conditions, describing to Irene his landlady's constant complaints about noise from late night study sessions with Jim, his roommate, and other classmates from Boston Tech. While there may very well have been some loud talk and laughter as the students worked their engineering problems, the landlady's displeasure, George and the others felt, was way out of proportion to their transgressions. With no K.A. chapter on campus, group study was one of the few social outlets open to George in Boston, and there were few places where the students could gather and socialize without disturbing non-student patrons or inhabitants. Boston Tech had not yet completed its dormitory, so most of the students had to live in various boarding houses in Boston, walking the mile over the Massachusetts Avenue Bridge to campus in Cambridge in all kinds of weather two to four times a day. In addition to the inconvenience of living off campus, the students' isolation prevented a strong college community from forming, and George greatly missed the camaraderie he had enjoyed at Georgia Tech.[42]

While George took exception to his landlady's complaints about the noise he and Jim made at night, his real quarrel with her arose over the issue of food. Jim's and George's boarding arrangement included breakfast, lunch, and dinner, and although George much later described the food as "pretty good—eggs, sausage, bacon, and toast for breakfast, soups and stews for lunch, and regular good food for dinner," his letters to Irene, written closer to the actual time of ingestion, painted a far grimmer picture.[43] "I don't know what we are going to do about this boarding house—it's going from bad to worse. The food is positively terrible; she had chicken for dinner today, and the odor was unbearable. I expect it had been dead for two months. It will be a miracle if both of us don't have ptomaine poisoning before we leave here."[44] The two young men apparently eventually made peace with the landlady and her menu, however, as they stayed at 263 Newbury Street for the duration of the academic year.

Woodruff's family missed him greatly while he was away at school, and there was a steady stream of advice and encouragement flowing to Boston by mail and telegram from 708 Edgewood Avenue in Atlanta. Soon after he was settled in his room at the boardinghouse, Emily Woodruff wrote to her son,

> I do trust and pray that you will associate with high class and moral boys at Boston Tech. . . . I told your father all about your experiences at Cornell and Princeton, and I think he will feel satisfied about you if you will make good, keep well, and beware of temptations and bad company. Be sure and take care of your money; spend it cautiously, get receipts for what you pay out, and send all the records to me.[45]

Ernest and Emily Woodruff's constant emphasis on careful accounting and good stewardship of financial resources made a lasting mark on George Woodruff. He thoroughly understood the value and proper management of money, and his keen eye for figures made him an invaluable member of the many boards he served throughout his lifetime, where he often played the role of watchdog over expenditures.

While Emily Woodruff was highly concerned with the suitability and moral character of her son's companions, the unfamiliar and, she thought, physically treacherous New England weather was as danger-

George W. Woodruff's bleak and much-maligned boardinghouse room at 263 Newbury Street in Boston. The TECHNOLOGY *flag stands for M.I.T.*

ous as bad company, and for that reason the topic occupied a good portion of her thoughts and her letters. Warnings to dress properly were interspersed regularly with news from home, along with repeated directives to purchase warmer long underwear and gloves immediately. Although Emily's worrying was at times maternally excessive, the bitterness of the Massachusetts winter did far surpass George's expectations. At the first snow, the magnitude of which amazed him, he found the rubbers that had protected him adequately from Atlanta's rains were no match for knee-deep Boston snows, particularly with the long walk to class every day. The hard-frozen Charles River was another shock, and George was unable to resist the temptation to walk across the ice to class, although one trip, accompanied by cracking sounds, was enough to satisfy his thirst for that particular adventure. High boots and a warmer overcoat were his first fall term purchases, and, following his parents' directions, he chose the items carefully and immediately sent the receipts home.[46]

Because Emily Woodruff had always channeled her full energy and concern into her husband, sons, and household, the periodic absence of three family members had a significant impact on her daily life. By 1916, Robert was married and on his own, George was in college and serious about Irene, and Henry also was rapidly approaching self-sufficiency. Even Ernest Woodruff was away from home regularly as business took him with increasing frequency to New York's financial center. Finding herself suddenly with fewer demands on her time and maternal expertise, Emily Woodruff occasionally expressed envy of Irene's unshakable hold on George's attention and affection. During Irene's second term at National Park, while George was still attending Georgia Tech, Emily wrote to her son from a vacation trip, "It makes me very jealous to think you miss Irene so much more than you do me. If I were at home, I expect you would be almost as lonely as you are now."[47] Despite her natural and predictable possessiveness toward her son, Emily was able to view George's loneliness objectively and offer wise advice in the best interest of both George and Irene. "You will make a mistake if you write Irene telling her that you are very miserable and lonely," she continued in her letter. "She will not get any good results from the school, and you should not get in the way of the opportunities that her father is giving her. Be a help to her, and not a drawback."[48]

Clara Belle King had even stronger feelings of jealousy over her daughter's attention, and Irene's letters to George were filled with dire warnings not to mention the frequency of their correspondence to her mother. Mrs. King, more direct in her approach than Mrs. Woodruff, often chided her daughter for writing to George first or more often than she wrote to her "own mother."[49] Clyde King also objected to what he perceived as their overly frequent correspondence, although for different reasons. Still feeling that Irene was too young to confine her social relationships to one person, Clyde King thought that if he could discourage his daughter from writing so regularly, he might be able to stave off an early marriage, an event he considered the inevitable result of steady and exclusive companionship.

Irene Tift King at age seventeen, taken upon entrance to National Park Seminary in Forest Glen, Maryland, in 1915.

Irene and George developed elaborate strategies to spare the Kings any worry over the regularity of their communication, trying to keep George in contact with the Kings, who liked him very much, without arousing any suspicion of an imminent marriage. "Go to see Mother sometime if you are not too busy," wrote Irene from National Park. "She would appreciate it and so would I, but if you go, for goodness's sake, don't mention my name."[50] When Irene returned to Atlanta for a vacation while George was still in Boston, the two struggled for several weeks to develop a plan that would allow them to write as often as they liked without being discovered. George proposed,

> . . . I'll write two, three, or as many letters as you say a week and address them to 1010 Ponce de Leon and address all the rest to some other place," George wrote. "Why don't I write to Buddie [brother Robert Woodruff] at the White Company with your letter in a separate envelope? He's the only one that could understand the situation and could have a messenger deliver it to you at any time and place you say. If you don't like this method, tell me some girl I could address it to."[51]

For a time at least, Nell Woodruff stepped in as "some girl" and received and delivered George's letters to Irene until the couple finally decided just to have all of the letters sent to the King home and meet parental questions as they came.[52]

George's and Irene's "situation," a plight mentioned frequently in both of their letters, was the seriousness of their relationship and the Kings' and Woodruffs' combined ignorance of their plans. Irene had promised her parents that she would not marry until she was twenty, and although she did not want to alarm them into thinking

Irene Tift King in 1916, while attending National Park Seminary in Forest Glen, Maryland.

she might deviate from her word, she often said that she wished her parents were aware of their plans so that she could talk openly with her mother without fearing she might reveal something she shouldn't.[53] George also often mused over his parents' probable reaction, writing to Irene, "If they only knew things as they really are, I wonder what they would say."[54]

While George and Irene did go to elaborate lengths to protect their parents from worry over their relationship, there is little doubt that the Woodruffs and the Kings understood far more than their offspring guessed. Soon after George enrolled at Boston Tech, Emily Woodruff and her sister Lizzie Winship Bates traveled to New York and Boston to visit George, shop, and see shows. While they were in Boston, they also took the opportunity to drive to Cambridge to find the graves of their great-great-great-great-grandparents, Edward and Rebecca Barham Winship, who had been buried in the churchyard across from the entrance of Harvard in 1717 and 1718.[55]

Aiming at subtlety, George urged his mother and Aunt Lizzie to visit Irene at National Park when they stopped to see Aunt Lizzie's daughter and Irene's good friend Annie Bates at Washington Seminary, telling her how much Irene would enjoy seeing her. Emily, however, intuiting the real reason for her son's request, wrote to him immediately upon her return, describing in minute detail Irene's clothes, hairstyle, facial expressions, mood, and conversational topics, adding generously at the end of her letter, "If I forgot anything, just ask."[56]

Ernest Woodruff also visited his son in Boston, although far more often he would telegraph George to join him for the weekend at the Waldorf-Astoria in New York. There, father and son would spend the day meeting with bankers and business executives involved with the elder Woodruff's various enterprises, and in the evenings, they would see shows and go to restaurants. It was the business meetings all day but study. . . . I do more in one day up here than I would in three at home."[67] He realized, however, that his ordeal was the price of a good education and endured it with relative stoicism. "You asked if I was glad I came here," George wrote. "Well, I'm glad in one respect, and in another, I'm not. I think I would have enjoyed life at Princeton much more than I do here, but I know I'm learning more here that I would at any other place, I don't care where it is."[68]

At M.I.T., the students took frequent field trips to learn about various areas of manufacturing, inspecting pump factories and touring the machine shops of the Boston Elevated Railroad, where they studied how the tracks were wired to carry the 6,000 volts necessary to run the trains.[69] George also joined the M.I.T. chapters of the Electrical Society and the American Society of Mechanical Engineers, and he attended their frequent programs and seminars with great enthusiasm.[70] While George was certainly interested in his studies and many activities for their own sake, he also saw this period of intense education as preparation for a more elevated calling. "When I leave here next June," he wrote to Irene toward the end of his first term, "I'll be ready to buck against the world, and to work for you until the end."[71]

Although George's commitment to his ultimate goal remained unswerving, outside forces soon intervened to change his immediate plans. He returned to M.I.T. after Christmas vacation in January of 1917 to the low rumblings of growing international disturbance, and as the country moved toward war, George Woodruff rose to meet new challenges and changes in plans.

ENDNOTES

¹Personal interview with Vela Rocker, George W. Woodruff's personal secretary (1959-1987), 5 September 1986.

²Personal interview with George W. Woodruff, 31 December 1985.

Letter, Irene Tift King to George W. Woodruff, 21 February 1916.

Letter, Irene Tift King to George W. Woodruff, 29 February 1916.

³*The Atlanta Journal,* "Clyde L. King Dies; Official of Plow Firm," 26 May 1941.

⁴"Mrs. Rushton At Last Rest," obituary in Irene King Woodruff's scrapbook, n.d., n.p., currently in the possession of her daughter, Jane Woodruff.

The Atlanta Journal, Winship obituary, 9 September 1899. Personal inerview with George W. Woodruff, 20 May 1986.

⁵Photographs of the Seven Mystic Maids are in Irene King Woodruff's personal collection, currently in the possession of her daughter, Jane Woodruff.

Telephone interview with Bertie Bond, Assistant to the President, Agnes Scott College, 30 September 1986.

⁶Clyde L. King obituary.

The Atlanta Journal or Constitution, "Plow Co. Great Asset to Area's Farm Life," c. 1946, found in Irene King Woodruff's scrapbook, in the possession of Jane Woodruff. Cf. "Fifty Years of Progress," King Plow Company promotional brochure c. 1952 in Irene King Woodruff's scrapbook, currently in the possession of her daughter, Jane Woodruff.

⁷Antoinette Johnson Matthews, *Oakdale Road: Atlanta, Ga., Dekalb County—Its History & Its People,* (Atlanta: n.p., 1972) 1. See, *The Atlanta Constitution,* "The Elegant Side of Ponce," 21 June 1979 and *The Atlanta Journal,* "Oakdale Road Tells Its Story," 19 October 1971.

⁸Matthews, *Oakdale Road,* viii. See also, *The Atlanta Constitution,* 21 June 1979 and *The Atlanta Journal,* 19 October 1971.

⁹*The Atlanta Constitution,* 21 June 1979.

Garrett, *Atlanta and Its Environs,* 2:526.

¹⁰Matthews, *Oakdale Road,* 1.

[11]Letter, George W. Woodruff to Irene Tift King 11 October 1916.

Letter, George W. Woodruff to Irene Tift King, 23 October 1916.

[12]Personal interview with George W. Woodruff, 25 July 1986.

[13]Letter, Irene Tift King to George W. Woodruff, 3 April 1917.

[14]Letter, Irene Tift King to George W. Woodruff, 6 April 1917.

[15]Letter, George W. Woodruff to Irene Tift King, 8 April 1917.

[16]Letter, Irene Tift King to George W. Woodruff, 14 April 1917.

[17]Letter, Irene Tift King to George W. Woodruff, 5 October 1916.

[18]Letter, George W. Woodruff to Irene Tift King, 19 February 1916.

[19]Letter, Irene Tift King to George W. Woodruff, 21 February 1916.

[20]Letter, Irene Tift King to George W. Woodruff, 7 February 1916.

[21]Personal interview with George W. Woodruff, 25 July 1986.

[22]Letter, Irene Tift King to Clara Belle Rushton King, 2 February 1916.

Letter, Irene Tift King to Clara Belle Rushton King, 1 February 1916.

[23]Letter, Irene Tift King to Clara Belle Rushton King, 2 February 1916.

[24]Letter, Irene Tift King to Clara Belle Rushton King, 1 February 1916.

Letter, Irene Tift King to George W. Woodruff, 10 March 1916.

[25]Letter, George W. Woodruff to Irene Tift King, 3 March 1916.

[26]Letter, George W. Woodruff to Irene Tift King, 25 April 1986.

[27]Letter, George W. Woodruff to Irene Tift King, 5 February 1916.

[28]Letter, George W. Woodruff to Irene Tift King, 26 March 1917.

[29]Pat Watters, *Coca-Cola: An Illustrated History* (Garden City, New York: Doubleday & Company, Inc., 1978) 130.

Personal interview with George W. Woodruff, 25 July 1986.

Letter, George W. Woodruff to Irene Tift King, 16 June 1916.

[30]Letter, George W. Woodruff to Irene Tift King, 16 June 1916.

[31]Letter, George W. Woodruff to Irene Tift King, 28 September 1916.

[32]Ibid.

[33]Letter, George W. Woodruff to Irene Tift King, 4 October 1916.

[34]Watters, *Coca-Cola*, 23.

[35]Letter, George W. Woodruff to Irene Tift King, 10 October 1916.

[36]Letter, George W. Woodruff to Irene Tift King, 6 March 1917.

[37]Letter, George W. Woodruff to Irene Tift King, 6 October 1916.

Letter, George W. Woodruff to Irene Tift King, 8 October 1916.

Letter, George W. Woodruff to Irene Tift King, 10 October 1916.

Letter, George W. Woodruff to Irene Tift King, 11 October 1916.

[38]Letter, George W. Woodruff to Irene Tift King, 2 November 1916.

Letter, George W. Woodruff to Irene Tift King, 12 October 1916.

[39]Letter, George W. Woodruff to Irene Tift King, 11 November 1916.

[40]Letter, George W. Woodruff to Irene Tift King, 6 October 1916.

Personal interview with George W. Woodruff, 3 January 1986.

⁴¹Letter, George W. Woodruff to Irene Tift King, 5 November 1916.

⁴²Letter, George W. Woodruff to Irene Tift King, 14 October 1916.

Letter, George W. Woodruff to Irene Tift King, 11 November 1916.

⁴³Personal interview with George W. Woodruff, 25 July 1986.

⁴⁴Letter, George W. Woodruff to Irene Tift King, 27 November 1916.

⁴⁵Letter, Emily Winship Woodruff to George W. Woodruff, 9 October 1916.

⁴⁶Personal interview with George W. Woodruff, 25 July 1986 and 7 October 1986.

⁴⁷Letter, Emily Winship Woodruff to George W. Woodruff, 5 February 1916.

⁴⁸Ibid.

⁴⁹Letter, Irene Tift King to George W. Woodruff, 4 April 1916.

Letter, Irene Tift King to George W. Woodruff, 9 April 1916.

⁵⁰Letter, Irene Tift King to George W. Woodruff, 3 February 1916.

⁵¹Letter, George W. Woodruff to Irene Tift King, 8 March 1916.

⁵²Letter, George W. Woodruff to Irene Tift King, 29 February 1916.

Letter, George W. Woodruff to Irene Tift King, 14 March 1917.

⁵³Letter, Irene Tift King to George W. Woodruff, 31 January 1917.

⁵⁴Letter, George W. Woodruff to Irene Tift King, 16 October 1916.

⁵⁵*The Genealogy of the Robert Winship Woodruff Family,* comp. Lucille Huffman (Atlanta: The Coca-Cola Company, 1973) 32.

⁵⁶Letter, Emily Winship Woodruff to George W. Woodruff, 21 October 1916.

⁵⁷Letter, George W. Woodruff to Irene Tift King, 26 February 1917.

Letter, George W. Woodruff to Irene Tift King, 19 April 1917.

⁵⁸Personal interviews with George W. Woodruff, 25 July 1986 and 7 October 1986.

⁵⁹Letter, George W. Woodruff to Irene Tift King, 3 November 1916.

⁶⁰Letter, Emily Winship Woodruff to George W. Woodruff, 12 October 1916.

Personal interview with George W. Woodruff, 7 October 1986.

⁶¹Letter, George W. Woodruff to Irene Tift King, 19 October 1916.

⁶²Letter, George W. Woodruff to Irene Tift King, 5 November 1916.

⁶³Letter, George W. Woodruff to Irene Tift King, 26 February 1917.

⁶⁴Personal interview with George W. Woodruff, 7 October 1986.

⁶⁵Letter, George W. Woodruff to Irene Tift King, 26 November 1916.

⁶⁶Letter, George W. Woodruff to Irene Tift King, 16 October 1916.

⁶⁷Letter, George W. Woodruff to Irene Tift King, 21 November 1916.

⁶⁸Letter, George W. Woodruff to Irene Tift King, 6 December 1916.

⁶⁹Letter, George W. Woodruff to Irene Tift King, 8 January 1917.

⁷⁰Letter, George W. Woodruff to Irene Tift King, 9 November 1916.

Letter, George W. Woodruff to Irene Tift King, 26 November 1916.

⁷¹Letter, George W. Woodruff to Irene Tift King, 6 December 1916.

Chapter Four
From Turmoil to Tranquility

By the time that George Woodruff returned to M.I.T. after Christmas of 1916, the situation in Europe had heated to an intolerable intensity. Woodruff took the train to New York on his way to Boston, and his car was filled with Atlantans traveling north to attend to business or go back to school. Most of the car's occupants knew each other, and the air was thick with vigorous discussions of the possibility of the United States' entrance into the war.[1] On his stopover in New York, Woodruff constantly came upon groups of men gathered on the sidewalks engaged in spirited debate of the issue. Upon his arrival in Boston, he found more of the same on the campus, and a bare two weeks after classes started, international events were coming to a head. "What do you think about the trouble we're having with Germany?" George wrote to Irene. "Everybody is terribly stirred up in this part of the country and thinks that war is inevitable. . . . It doesn't look good, . . . and [it] is enough to start a man thinking seriously."[2]

On January 31, 1917, rankling at Britain's continuing naval blockade, Germany declared a second unrestricted submarine campaign against England, disregarding the fact that its first such campaign had been halted at the insistence of President Wilson in April of 1916. Citing the ruthlessness and meager results of the first siege, the United States demanded that Germany's plan for a second submarine effort be aborted as well. When the German government refused to yield to President Wilson's ultimatum, the United States cut all diplomatic ties with the country on February 3, 1917, ending the official neutrality that had been proclaimed by the president two and a half years earlier.

George Woodruff, appropriately alarmed at the turn of events and, as he wrote in a letter, "sick with actual pains" from missing Irene, struggled to gather as much information as he could about the country's expectations of its combat-aged citizens. As the situation grew more tense, he realized that even his status as an M.I.T. student could place him in a special position regarding an eventual draft. "This German situation is getting worse and worse," George wrote two days after relations with Germany were severed. He continued,

> American officers have already taken complete possession of German ships in Boston Harbor and have sent the German crews to the immigration island. Everybody around school says that if war is declared we will be among the first to be called, on account of our military department.[3]

Several days later, George, while understandably ambivalent about his special vulnerability to the draft, praised his university's readiness for action: "The spirit up here is something for the country to be proud of; the whole school building and all apparatus has been offered to the government, and in the case of war, it will be put into immediate service."[4]

While many United States citizens may have been angered by what they perceived as President Wilson's excess of patience with the Germans during the two year period of official neutrality, the end result of the United States' restraint was a large consolidation of opinion favoring intervention in the war. The Germans' deliberate sinking of the British ship *Lusitania* with a loss of 128 American lives and their intense efforts to instigate action against the United States by Mexico were among the many provocations endured over the two-year period, and the American people were largely unified in their determination that the United States not be further challenged. Although Woodruff shared his country's resolve on that score, he was also concerned about what would happen to Irene should the United States declare war and send troops overseas. For the approximately three-month period between the severing of diplomatic ties with Germany and the passage of the conscription bill in May of 1917, Woodruff, like so many other young men his age, did his best to balance patriotism with personal commitment and find the branch of military service that would allow him to serve his country while remaining as close to home as possible.

Five days after diplomatic ties were severed, Woodruff reported that mass meetings were being held every day in Boston and also on campus, and even the president of M.I.T. spoke out at one rally in favor of the students' immediate enlistment. By the time Woodruff wrote to Irene of the rallies, great numbers of his classmates had already followed their academic leader's suggestion, caught up in the patriotic fervor sweeping the nation.[5] For those students who had not yet enlisted, there were slips of paper posted all over campus for them to sign indicating their preferred branch of service, and petitions were circulated asking for support of mandatory military training and compulsory service for young men under twenty.[6]

Ernest Woodruff, always interested in and protective of his second son, immediately became involved in the unfolding drama. George reported regularly to Irene that he had received yet another letter from his father filled with detailed instructions outlining how he should meet various contingencies as they might arise. Ernest cautioned George strongly to be on his guard in attending mass meetings of any kind, saying that it was easy to be carried along by the spirit of the crowd and enlist in a certain branch of service without fully thinking out the decision. If war was declared, the elder Woodruff said, George did not necessarily have to return to Atlanta immediately. If, however, the German fleet went out to sea, George was to telegraph his father the moment he heard the news and get on the next train to Atlanta. "If this should happen, and it is very improbable," George then wrote to Irene, *"you will return with me."*[7]

In the weeks that followed, international tension continued to escalate steadily, and by late March of 1917, Boston's streets were filled with marching infantry and cavalry. Both exhilarated and wary at the growing air of militarism, George wrote to Irene, "Things up here are all excitement, . . . and everybody seems to be in a hurry. Quite a few fellows over at school are in the reserves in their home towns and are expecting to be called at any minute."[8] Feeling that East Coast cities were especially at risk should the German navy penetrate the United States' blockade, Ernest Woodruff wrote to his son, urgently instructing him to get out of Boston immediately in the case of such an eventuality, buying a motorcycle if necessary to ride inland as quickly as possible.[9] While Ernest Woodruff's advice might otherwise have seemed overly alarmist, the atmosphere around Boston did little to diminish George's concern. "There are troops guarding every bridge between New York and Boston," he wrote to Irene two days after war was declared. "Somebody tried to blow up the bridge over the Charles last night, which necessitated quite a little battle. It was the first shooting the Boston guardsmen have had. Did you ever imagine that Easter Sunday would bring the sad tidings of an almost worldwide war?"[10]

On April 6, 1917, war against Germany, Austria, and Hungary was finally declared, and a call went up for volunteers. The pressure on M.I.T. students to enlist then reached a new high as school officials warned that the country's inevitable resort to the draft would put a quick end to any chance of receiving a commission or expressing a preference as to division or branch of service.[11] As he wrote to Irene in early April, "if I go [overseas], it will not be because I want to, but because it is my duty as an American to fight for my country."[12]

While he was not unwilling to go into combat service, George hoped to find an area of the military where he could use his technological education, and he examined his options carefully, considering a variety of different opportunities. He leaned heavily toward the Officers Reserve Corps of the Coast Artillery for a period of time, reasoning that he would be able to make his electrical and mechanical engineering training useful there and would also probably be stationed in the United States. He began studying seriously for the officer's exam but was interrupted in the middle of his task by a visit from his brother and sister-in-law, Robert and Nell Woodruff. Robert convinced his brother to postpone any irreversible action until he was able to check the availability of civilian commissions in the Atlanta area, and George then decided to stay in Boston until the end of the term unless hostilities developed to a point where it would be safer to be at home. Nell, however, apparently unaware of the brothers' agreement, casually related George's original plan to Ernest Woodruff, who, aside from his desire to see his son finish school, was vehemently opposed to any decision in which he had exercised no influence. Ernest was predictably displeased with the idea of the Coast Artillery and sent off what George later described to Irene as "a very strong letter," begging to know why his son had not considered his wishes. George wrote to Irene several days later, however, his mind eased at the receipt of a friendly letter from his father enclosing a big check. "Evidently he isn't mad any longer, but I'm expecting some argument when we get together," George wrote with both humor and relief.[13]

Irene too felt the effects of the war at school in Maryland, as her home nursing course suddenly switched its emphasis to surgical dressings, and home cooking evolved into Red Cross dietetics. Irene wrote enthusiastically of making bandages for the Red Cross in the evenings, studying for her Red Cross certification in dietetics and nursing, and applying for a position at the Red Cross headquarters in Washington. "If the war gets bad," she wrote to George in early April, "I have no intention of staying at home."[14]

Emily Woodruff was faithful in keeping George informed of the Atlanta boys' military activities, hoping that their experiences and considerations might help him to reach an informed decision. While lamenting that she "certainly did not raise boys to fight," she reported his friends' whereabouts, nothing that his former classmates at Georgia Tech were going to graduate early and be sent directly to Fort McPherson.[15] "There will not be any dances or entertainments of any kind at the close of school this year," Emily wrote, "as so many of the boys have gone in training."[16] After driving out to Fort McPherson to look at the newly built barracks, she reported to George, "it will be rough living, . . . and the experiences the boys are having are very hard. . . . I do hope my boys will never have such hardships."[17]

In Boston, the reality of war continued to be far more immediate than bandages, dietetics exams, and hastily-built barracks. By mid-April, U.S. patrol boats were guarding Boston Harbor from every angle, and no ships of any nationality were allowed in or out of the harbor after sunset. Rumors were circulating to the effect that Germany was attempting to create a submarine blockade of all of the United States' large ports, and there was an attempt to dynamite the wharves in Boston Harbor, averted only when a telephone operator overheard the plot and notified authorities.[18] The conscription bill was close to being passed, which only intensified the efforts of the young men of draft age to find their best military options. George continued his correspondence with his brother Robert and his father, trying to fin-

Emily Winship Woodruff in about 1912.

ish his school term while maintaining his range of choice in service as the compulsory draft became a reality. Robert, who had been commissioned as a captain in the Ordnance Department of the United States Army in January of 1918, had connections with the Quartermaster's Department in Atlanta, and George was very interested in the possibility of service in that area. He was also considering the officers' training program at Fort McPherson, which, however, was to start long before the academic year's end. As the deadline for application to the officers' training program drew near, George finally decided to finish out his term at school, gambling that he would not be drafted in the meantime and that Robert would be successful in securing him a position in the Quartermaster's Department or in an industry in government service.[19]

Irene graduated from National Park Seminary in the middle of May, and George finished his junior year at M.I.T., returning to Atlanta in June. While waiting for an opportunity in civilian service or a war industry, George joined the Emory Medical Corps, where his responsibility was to transport doctors and medical supplies around the Emory campus and back and forth to Fort McPherson on an Army motorcycle with a sidecar.[20] Mandatory military service made George's return to M.I.T. in the fall impossible, so he stayed on in the medical corps for about eight months, until Ernest Woodruff, frustrated at the military's slowness in finding George a position that made use of his technical education, traveled to Washington to have a word with officials in the War Department about the delay. The best use of a man with a mechanical education, Ernest pointed out with righteous insistence, was in an industry filling government contracts, not driving a motorcycle with a sidecar through the streets of Atlanta. An appropriately short time after Ernest's Washington visit, George was notified of an available position in the Terry Shipbuilding Company in Savannah, Georgia, and the Woodruffs and Irene put George on the train to that coastal city on March 8, 1918.[21]

While George had hoped that the change to the Terry Shipbuilding Company would mean an engineering position that would draw upon his technological training, the job he was initially assigned to do at the shipyard turned out to be a grave disappointment. Writing to Irene soon after his arrival in Savannah, George complained,

> [They have] put me out on the ships carrying steel plates and angles weighing from fifty to one hundred pounds each. I have to bolt them in place and mark them, and at odd times I have to walk all over the yard looking for misplaced steel. My job at present is what is termed in the army as hard labor. . . . It's awful—it's terrible—but it's better than the army.[22]

Irene worried constantly about his long hours, loneliness, and hard work, but wrote with especial frequency cautioning him about his red Indian motorcycle, which the Woodruffs had sent to him on the train from Atlanta to use on the long ride out to the shipyard.[23] George rode every morning from his room in the Savannah Hotel to the shipyard, and Irene, knowing her fiance, was diligent in her exhortations that he should drive safely and slowly, particularly after he was reprimanded by a Savannah policeman for speeding.[24]

By the time that Irene and George were once again separated by George's move to Savannah, their plans for the future had been set and announced to family and friends, George had given Irene an engagement ring, and all that remained to do was announce a date. With their announcement, the couple joined many of their friends in rushing to get married before the men were sent overseas or posted far from home in the United States, and Irene often wrote to George of Sundays spent sewing trousseaux for roommates in school and friends at home in Atlanta. After two years apart while they were away at school, Irene and George were unwilling to accept another separation of uncertain duration, so they began planning to get married as soon as possible so that Irene could join George in Savannah. Because Irene had long before promised her parents that she would not marry until she turned twenty, however, the wedding could not take place until after George took his post at the shipyard, and his rigorous schedule with the shipbuilding company threatened at first to further complicate their plans. Good fortune prevailed, however, and hasty preparations began for a wedding on April 17, 1918, the day after Irene's twentieth birthday.[25]

Wedding invitation for the marriage of Irene Tift King and George W. Woodruff on April 17, 1918.

> Mr. and Mrs. Clyde Lanier King
>
> request the pleasure of your company
>
> at the marriage of their daughter
>
> Irene Tift
>
> to
>
> Mr. George Waldo Woodruff
>
> on Wednesday, the seventeenth of April
>
> at nine o'clock in the evening
>
> Ten hundred ten Ponce de Leon Avenue
>
> Atlanta, Georgia

When the wedding date was announced, Mrs. King nearly went into shock at the realization that there remained only a month to complete all of the necessary preparations for the event. As the groom's parents, Emily and Ernest Woodruff had far less to worry about between the announcement and the wedding and consequently were unreservedly delighted by the impending marriage. Emily even teased Irene with somewhat uncharacteristic humor that her years of toil were only beginning. "I've spoiled George for almost twenty-three years," she said good-naturedly. "Now it's your turn." Irene's parents, however, faced with the myriad tasks a wedding creates, did not receive their daughter's announcement with the Woodruffs' equanimity. "When I told my parents that we wanted the wedding on the seventeenth, they both nearly died and acted as if I really meant what I was talking about for the first time," Irene wrote to George several weeks after he left for Savannah. "They tried to argue me out of it, but I wouldn't be argued, so they had to give in."[26]

Before a wedding suitable for the eldest daughter of a prominent family could be held in the Kings' home, there were floors to be refinished, new draperies to be made, invitations, stationery, calling cards, and flowers to be ordered; and ribbon bearers, train bearers, ring bearers, flower girls, bridesmaids, and all of their clothing and accessories to be organized. Necessity quickly overcame panic, however, and Irene and her mother attacked their task with zeal. Irene's letters to George were filled with the names of prospective bridesmaids and groomsmen, suggested gifts for attendants, guest lists, and fabric samples, and as she discussed all of the various design decisions to be made in connection with the upcoming festivities, such as what shade of shoes would look best with light green taffeta, she would frequently add, "I don't know if you know what I'm talking about or not—but if you do, do you think it would be pretty?"[27]

Like most brides, Irene was ambivalent about all of the excitement. "I surely wish you were here to help with all these things," she wrote after a successful day of shopping. "You are missing the fun of the wedding."[28] After several days of confusion and frustration, however, her view of the situation had changed: "I'll be so thankful when the whole thing is over. . . . Mother and I will both be just dead."[29] Despite Irene's exhausted lament, she and George both obviously enjoyed all of the preparations for their long-awaited wedding. It was the very cause of their exhaustion—invitation lists, menu plans, flowers, trousseaux, congratulations, presents, and Irene's new monogram—that kept them conscious that the wedding they had planned for so long was an imminent reality. Said Irene of her incredulity, "We have been putting this thing off for so long, I just can't believe that it is really about to happen."[30] George too was relishing his impending change in status, writing to Irene of the teasing he was getting from his friends at the shipyard and of their new landlord's frequent references to "his wife": "You should have heard Mr. Rossignol referring to you as *Mrs. Woodruff* yesterday. It sure did sound fine."[31]

The year before their wedding plans became finalized, Irene and George had entered into a teasing argument over whether Irene would ever be addressed as *Mrs. Woodruff* when she rotated into the position of hostess in her cooking class. It was the custom at National Park for the students serving as cook, chambermaid, and waitress to be called by their first names, while the girl serving as hostess would be addressed by the honorific *Mrs.* combined with a surname of the other girls' choosing. Knowing Irene's longstanding relationship with George, Irene's classmates immediately dubbed her *Mrs. Woodruff* and then dared her to sign her name that way in her next letter to George. Irene took the dare, but then begged George in her letter to of widows and orphans of Ireland's sons who have died or been injured in the war. On their recent visit to Belfast, Lady Carson shared with her husband the enthusiastic greetings of the people.

* * *

Buffet Supper For Bridal Party

Mr. and Mrs. Ernest Woodruff entertained Monday evening at a buffet supper at their home in Inman Park, in compliment to Miss Irene King and Mr. George Woodruff, whose marriage will be a brilliant event of Wednesday evening.

In the drawing room, where the guests were received, the mantels had tall vases of pink carnations and purple iris. In the dining room the table had as its center decoration a large silver basket filled with pink carnations. Silver candlesticks held pink-shaded candles, and the mints and bonbons were in pink and white. On the mantel was a large basket filled with Easter lilies.

Mr. and Mrs. Woodruff were assisted in entertaining by Mr. and Mrs. Robert Woodruff.

Mrs. Woodruff was handsomely gowned in black Georgette crepe embroidered in beads.

Miss King wore orchid-colored Georgette over silver cloth.

The guests included the wedding party and the out-of-town guests.

* * *

Trail Travelers

The Trail Travelers' Bible study class will hold its regular meeting at the residence of Mrs. B. E. Hudson, 46 Penn avenue, Tuesday morning at 10 o'clock. Mrs. Treadwell, leader.

Atlanta Journal, April 1918.

tear up the embarrassing manuscript on sight, explaining the bet and vowing that she would never sign her name like that again. In his next letter, George teased back, "Regarding the bet, the explanation was very full and was understood perfectly, but don't you make a kind of a broad statement when you said you would never sign your name that way again?"[32] Touched, Irene responded, "I guess maybe I did . . . but I don't guess I ever will sign another letter that way to you."[33]

While Irene probably never did find another occasion to sign *Mrs. Woodruff* at the close of a letter to George, she formally adopted his name as her own on the evening of April 17, 1918, before hundreds of friends and family members from Atlanta and beyond. The wedding of George Waldo Woodruff and Irene Tift King took place at nine o'clock on a cool, moonlit spring night in the Kings' home at 1010 Ponce de Leon Avenue. Arriving guests walked up the path through the cool darkness to the house, warmed first visually by the sight of the festive lighting and then actually by the excitement and hospitality within.[34]

The house was decorated with huge baskets and bowls of deep pink peonies on tables and stands, and baskets of roses, sweet peas, Easter lilies, and lilies of the valley hung everywhere. The sun porch and other outer rooms had been trimmed with garlands of smilax and enclosed with canvas against the cool night, and the verandahs were dotted with hundreds of pink-shaded electric light bulbs. In addition to the hanging electric bulbs, the rooms were lit with dozens of candles, whose light glowed warmly over the pale green taffeta gowns of the bridesmaids. Clara Belle, Irene's younger sister and maid of honor, was dressed in pink organdy and hand-made lace, as were the flower girls and ribbon bearers. Four-year-old John, the youngest King child, was dressed in a white satin suit to carry out his duties as ring bearer.[35]

All of the girls carried pink sweet peas, the bridesmaids in bouquets and the flower girls in baskets, while Irene, feeling regal in the white satin gown she had designed to incorporate lace from her mother's wedding dress, carried a full cascade of lilies of the valley. Her veil also had been worn twenty-four years earlier by Clara Belle King, although Irene fashioned it differently, gathering it onto a small wreath of fresh orange blossoms. Because her dress was ornately beaded with tiny pearls, she had originally decided against wearing any jewelry, but George surprised her with a wedding gift, a diamond bar pin set in platinum, and Irene proudly fastened it to her neckline.

A small orchestra played softly until the ceremony began and then drew attention to Irene, her father, and her attendants as they made their entrance by way of the wide central staircase, walking past the flower trimmed banister and through the guests to reach George and his brother Henry, the best man, in front of the altar in the living room. The wedding then took place under a large four leaf clover-

Irene Tift King and her bridesmaids, taken at the wedding of Irene Tift King and George Waldo Woodruff on April 17, 1918. Mr. and Mrs. Woodruff were married in the home of Mrs. Woodruff's parents, Mr. and Mrs. Clyde Lanier King, at 1010 (later renumbered 1386) Ponce de Leon Avenue, now the Alpha Delta Pi Sorority's Memorial Headquarters. Mrs. Woodruff turned twenty the day before the wedding. Mr. Woodruff was twenty-two and had just begun work in a shipyard in Savannah as a civilian alternative to military service. The Woodruffs celebrated sixty-four wedding anniversaries prior to Mrs. Woodruff's death on December 25, 1982. Left to right in the photograph are Frances Winship, George Woodruff's first cousin; Fannie Watlington, Clara Belle King, Mrs. Woodruff's younger sister; Irene King Woodruff, Hazel Mayer, and Kate Woolfolk, a friend of Mrs. Woodruff's from National Park Seminary.

shaped canopy made of roses, swansonia, and Easter lilies and twinkling all over with tiny electric lights.[36] After the ceremony was concluded, the guests ate, drank, cut wedding cake, and danced, showering Irene and George with rice from tiny satin slippers and rose petals from pink tulle sacks as they set out on their honeymoon.

Their destination was New York City, although Irene, loving intrigue, had made George promise not to tell anyone where they were going. "Let's keep it a deep, dark secret and not tell a soul," she wrote to George several weeks before the wedding. "Everybody has been asking about it, but I tell them I have no idea of telling them."[37] At the last minute, George, expecting to have only three days away from the shipyard, had been pleasantly surprised with ten days of leave, so the newlyweds had a full week in New York for sightseeing, enjoying various hotels' restaurants, and attending the theater in the evenings. They returned to Atlanta by train during the last week of April and packed their wedding presents and Lizzie, the King family cook, into their brand new Buick, a wedding gift from the Woodruffs. They then departed for Savannah to set up housekeeping.[38]

George and Irene Woodruff moved into a little bungalow at 1209 Forty-ninth Street that George had leased for six months at $47 per month from Charles P. Rossignol of the Parkside Land Company in Savannah.[39] Irene was charmed by the house's little porch, and by June, the yard was in full bloom. "It's just like a country home," George wrote to Irene while she was on a brief trip back to Atlanta in July to pack up more wedding gifts. "It is *way* out [of Savannah, and] the yard, garden, and flowers are *much* prettier than I thought. Most of the roses and flowers are in full bloom, and from the outside, the place is *beautiful*."[40]

In addition to the beauty it brought to their little yard, the summer also saw a change for the better for George at the shipyard, as the shipbuilding company finally moved him into a position as a draftsman soon after his return from New York. George spent the remainder of his time with the company busy at his draftsman's table, making mechanical drawings of the ships that were built in the yard. He took the basic designs he was given and rendered them into explicit plans and scale drawings for the shops to follow in actually building the steel-framed, wood-hulled ships.[41]

Throughout their stay in Savannah, Irene occupied herself around the house, delighting in knitting, sewing, polishing silver and arranging her household, as well as driving around town and out to the shipyard to visit George in the new Buick. Lizzie, who came to help set up housekeeping, returned to Atlanta after a month, as the house was small enough for Irene to care for herself. In mid-September, when the weather began to cool, George and Irene moved to an apartment in town, and George continued as a draftsman at the shipyard until the war's end in November of 1918. At that point, although it would have been feasible to plan to return to M.I.T. in January to be-

14 THE ATLANTA JOURNAL

Mr. Geo. W. Woodruff Weds Miss Irene King

THE marriage of Miss Irene Tift King and Mr. George W. Woodruff was solemnized Wednesday evening at 9 o'clock at the home of the bride's parents, Mr. and Mrs. Clyde Lanier King, on Ponce de Leon avenue, the Rev. Theron Rice and the Rev. Richard Orme Flinn officiating.

Several hundred guests were assembled to witness the marriage of this popular young couple. The ceremony was performed in the large living room of the handsome home, where tropical plants and ferns were banked high to the ceiling, interspersed with snowy clusters of Easter lilies and peonies. A canopy, in the shape of a four-leaf clover, formed entirely of lilies, smilax and jeweled with tiny electric lights, was suspended over the wedding party. Brass candelabra, holding tall cathedral lights, placed on white pedestals, flanked the altar on each side.

The other rooms where the guests assembled were adorned with peonies and lilies, and the spacious porches canvased in and converted into tropical gardens were illuminated with rose-shaded lights.

Bridal Party

Miss Clara Belle King, a sister of the bride, who was the maid of honor, wore a quaint gown of pink organdie and carried an old-fashioned bouquet of pink sweetpeas.

The bridesmaids, including Miss Frances Winship, Miss Fannie Watlington, Miss Hazel Myers, of Dayton, Ohio, and Miss Kate Woolfolk, of Columbus, were gowned in green taffeta and tulle and carried cascade bouquets of pink sweetpeas with green streamers.

Little Miss Ethel Woodruff, of Columbus and Miss Ella B. Huffman, the flower girls, wore dainty frocks of pink organdie and pink ribbons, and their baskets were filled with pink sweet peas.

Sarah Hurt, Jennie Hodgson, Mary McCarty, Elinor McGinty, Mollie Wight Harrell, Estelle Boynton, Clayton Callaway and Lucile Stone, the little ribbon bearers, wore pink organdie and taffeta combined.

Master John King, the three-year-old brother of the bride, was the ring-bearer, and little Annie Huffman was the train-bearer.

Mr. Henry Woodruff was the best man and the groomsmen included Captain Robert Woodruff, Mr. Don Watts, of Chicago; Mr. William Moore, Mr. Albert Pritchard and Mr. Kenneth Dunwoody.

The Bride

The bride, who was given in marriage by her father, Mr. Clyde L. King, was lovely in her bridal robes of white satin and tulle and rare lace, which had been worn by her mother at her wedding. The tulle veil was held in place by a chaplet of orange blossoms and her flowers were a cascade bouquet of valley lilies tied with airy white tulle.

Following the ceremony an elegant reception was held. The receiving party included Mr. and Mrs. Ernest Woodruff, Mrs. R. H. Huffman, Miss Margaret Rushton, Mrs. Charles Winship, Mrs. Elizabeth Winship Bates, Mrs. George Walters, Mrs. A. P. Coles, Mrs. W. F. Wilson, Mrs. Andrew Bramlett, of Charleston, S. C., Mrs. B. J. King, of LaGrange, Mrs. William Rushton, Mrs. James Dougherty, Mrs. William Bedell, of Chattanooga, Tenn.; Mrs. Thomas Joseph Walsh, of New York, Mrs. Henry Heinz, Mrs. George Hurt, Mrs. George Brine, Mrs. A. E. Harless, Mrs. Frank Dean, Mrs. William E. Campbell, Mrs. Charles Boynton and Mrs. Clayton Callaway.

Mrs. King, the mother of the bride, was handsomely gowned in white satin and tulle effectively combined, and Mrs. Ernest Woodruff, the mother of the groom, wore an elegant gown of white Georgette crepe elaborately embroidered in white and silver threads.

Miss Elizabeth Hawkins, Miss Laura Sawtell and Miss Virginia Collier served punch.

The bride's table, arranged in the breakfast room, was converted into a beautiful Italian garden. The center of the elaborately appointed table was decorated with miniature marble statues grouped amongst velvety moss, in the midst of which played a white marble fountain. Small urns held tiny pink rose bushes and valley lilies.

An artistic canopy of lights and flowers and ribbons of rose shaded lights extending to the corners of the room was suspended overhead. From the center of the canopy was hung a basket of pink roses and lilies illuminated with tiny pink lights.

A wedding cake built in tiers surmounted with the Tower of Love holding cupid figures, was placed at one end of the table. Ribbon streamers radiating from the lower tier to the places of the bridal party were drawn for the wedding souvenirs.

The bride's gifts to her attendants were gold thimbles and to the little ribbon bears she gave gold bracelets.

Rose petals contained in pink tulle bags were showered on the bride and groom before their departure.

Mr. and Mrs. Woodruff left for a wedding trip after which they will make their future home in Savannah, where Mr. Woodruff is engaged in ship building for the government.

Among the out-of-town guests present were Mr. and Mrs. B. J. King, of LaGrange; Mrs. Andrew Bramlett, of Charleston; Mr. and Mrs. Harry Murphy, of New York; Miss Hazel Myers, of Dayton, Ohio; Miss Kate Woolfolk, of Columbus, Ga.; Mr. Donald Watts, of Chicago.

* * *

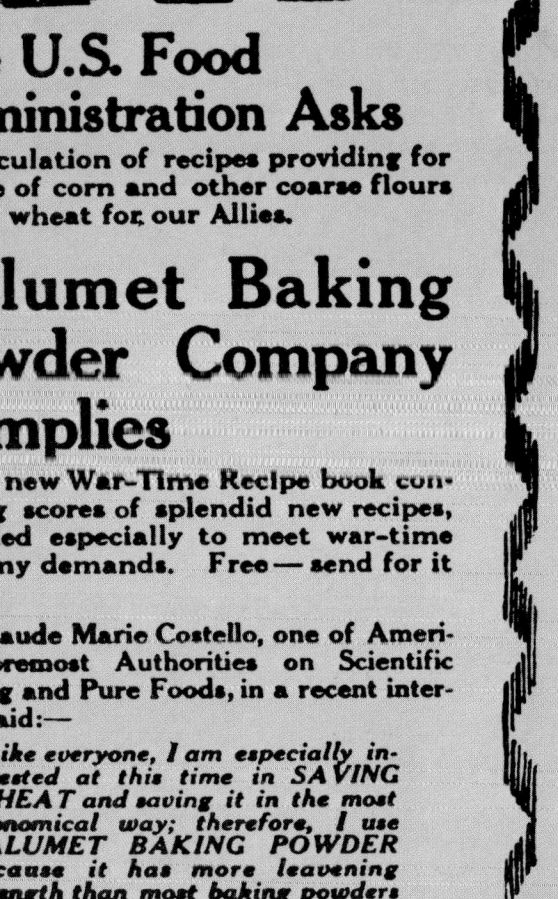

The U.S. Food Administration Asks

the circulation of recipes providing for the use of corn and other coarse flours to save wheat for our Allies.

Calumet Baking Powder Company Complies

With a new War-Time Recipe book containing scores of splendid new recipes, compiled especially to meet war-time economy demands. Free — send for it today.

Miss Maude Marie Costello, one of America's foremost Authorities on Scientific Cooking and Pure Foods, in a recent interview, said:—

"Like everyone, I am especially interested at this time in SAVING WHEAT and saving it in the most economical way; therefore, I use CALUMET BAKING POWDER because it has more leavening strength than most baking powders

Atlanta Journal, April 1918.

1925 side view of the Oakdale Road home picturing the Woodruffs' much loved 1918 Buick, given to them as a wedding gift by Woodruff's parents, Ernest and Emily Woodruff.

gin his last year of study, his marriage and his success as a draftsman at the shipbuilding company made that option less attractive than staying out in the working world. As soon as he was able to leave the shipbuilding company after the end of the war, George secured a job as a draftsman for Atlantic Steel, and George and Irene then returned to Atlanta, renting a small apartment in the Blackmon Building at 371 Ponce de Leon Avenue between the old Sears and Boulevard Street.[42]

Longtime Woodruff family friend Thomas K. Glenn was the president of Atlantic Steel when George signed on as a draftsman, having been recruited for the position when Ernest Woodruff reorganized the Steel Company's management in 1907.[43] During the years of Glenn's presidency, the company had gone through a period of steady growth, and the board of directors had voted to reincorporate Atlantic Steel in Delaware in 1915. The new corporation was domesticated in Georgia at that time, and its success continued through and beyond the busy years of World War I, despite some small difficulties in the first few years following the war.

While George very much enjoyed returning to Atlantic Steel in a permanent capacity, his new responsibilities were very different from the summer jobs he had held while he was in school. During summers, he had worked in the efficiency department, where he was able to use much of the knowledge and skill he was acquiring in the shops of Tech High, Georgia Tech, and M.I.T. in making timed studies of the company's nail machines, drilling presses, and other manufacturing equipment.[44] In his work as a draftsman, he continued to employ his technological education, using knowledge acquired over years spent in mechanical drawing classes and shops, as well as experience gained with the Terry Shipbuilding Company in Savannah. Although the industry at the Steel Company was vastly different from shipbuilding and George was responsible for drafting plans for new equipment designs and machine overhauls rather than ships' hulls, the basic principles of the draftsman were the same, and George settled easily and happily into his work. He was delighted to be back in Atlanta, and he enjoyed his co-workers and the camaraderie of the engineers and draftsmen at the plant, particularly admiring Cliff Coles, the Steel Company's chief engineer. He was also very much aware of

Advertisement for Atlantic Ice & Coal, where George Woodruff worked as a retail ice salesman while in high school and college and as an engineer from 1919 to 1920.

Tom Glenn's presence as president of the company, but he kept a friendly, respectful distance from the older man, determined to demonstrate his competence as a draftsman without reference to his father's or Mr. Glenn's role in the company.[45]

Although George was challenged by his work at Atlantic Steel, drafting did little to satisfy his longtime love for machines and mechanics, so there was no time spent in debate over whether to take an engineering position at the Atlantic Ice & Coal Company when it became available in early 1919. Atlantic Ice & Coal was another of the companies where George had worked during his summer vacations, cutting and selling ten pound blocks of ice for a nickel apiece on the retail sales dock at the plant. While retail sales had not overly stimulated George's interest or used his training, George enjoyed his time at Atlantic Ice & Coal and seized the engineering opportunity eagerly, knowing he would enjoy the people and the work. He was shortly traveling to thirty-four different ice plants all over Georgia, Florida, Alabama, and Tennessee, running batteries of tests on engines and coal-run boilers to make certain they were operating safely and efficiently. It was the coal-fueled boilers that produced the steam necessary to compress ammonia, the chemical agent used to cool the water contained in the huge cans in which the 300 pound blocks of ice were frozen.

After George made several trips to the ice plants alone, he and Irene decided that they did not want to be separated while he was on the road, so they traveled together across the Southeast in their Buick, staying in hotels in the towns where the ice plants were located for the week at a time necessary to fully test each plant's equipment. During the day while George was at work, Irene would knit and sew in her hotel room, lonely but glad at least to be in the same town as her new husband.[46] When the testing was completed, George would spend a short time writing a report to the chief engineer, and the two would then move on to the next ice plant.

Later in 1919, after George had been working for several months with the Atlantic Ice & Coal Company, an event took place that would one day make the Woodruff family, as well as many other Atlantans, very rich. During the summer of that year, Ernest Woodruff entered into the largest corporate acquisition he had yet or would ever mastermind. After forming a syndicate consisting of the Trust Company of Georgia, the Chase National Bank, and the Guaranty Trust Company of New York, Ernest Woodruff arranged the purchase of The Coca-Cola Company from Asa G. Candler's wife and five children for $25,000,000, an amount that seemed exorbitant at the time, but soon proved to be a small investment in a very lucrative future.[47] The Coca-Cola Company's staggering growth and success, one of Atlanta's and the nation's most brilliant combinations of leadership, luck, and an ideal mass market product, was eventually to increase the wealth of many Atlantans beyond their wildest imaginations and provide the philanthropic capital to bring the city and the region to an impressive level in educational, medical, and cultural facilities.

"Dr." John Styth Pemberton, a pharmacist and manufacturer of patent medicines, invented the base syrup for Coca-Cola in 1886. The product's good taste and the timely intervention in the naming process by Pemberton's partner, Frank M. Robinson, saved the new invention from joining the obscure ranks of Pemberton's many other short-lived medicinal concoctions. Pemberton, not unlike other men of his time and trade, was endowed with a late nineteenth century patent medicine man's affection for grand claims and had an unsuppressible predilection for imaginative and exotic-sounding names for his products. Robinson, however, was a bookkeeper by trade and infinitely more practical and progressive in his marketing strategies than his druggist partner. After thinking a moment, he dubbed the promising nostrum "Coca-Cola" after two of the product's ingredients, the coca bean and the kola nut. Unlike some of Pemberton's other creations—Pemberton's Globe of Flower Cough Syrup, Pemberton's French Wine of Coca, and Pemberton's Extract of Styllinger ("For the Blood")—Coca-Cola sounded neither like a medicine nor a mysterious potion, and Robinson further boosted the syrup's future by sitting down to pen in his fluid bookkeeper's script the trademark that is famous today. For the sake of symmetry, Robinson made the decision to spell *kola* with a *C*, rightly thinking that the pair of *C's* would be attractive in advertising.[48]

Pemberton and Robinson sold the first glass of Coca-Cola as it is known today in May of 1886 from the counter of Jacobs' Drug Store, a favorite local gathering place on the southwest corner of Peachtree and Marietta Streets, where the First National Bank Tower now stands. The way in which the syrup evolved from yet another questionable potion created by a local druggist into a world-famous beverage is a subject of a great body of myth and legend. The one constant in all of the stories is that Pemberton originally intended for the syrup to be drunk plain or mixed with tap water, and the addition of carbonated water was a very fortuitous accident. One of the most popular and probably most accurate stories of the beverage's creation is that Pemberton arrived at Jacobs' with a gallon jug of Coca-Cola syrup under his arm and somehow persuaded Dr. Jacobs, the proprietor of the pharmacy, and the soda fountain operator to try the syrup mixed with plain water and ice. They liked the drink and reached for second helpings, this time, however, using the hydrant for carbonated water by mistake, and their imaginations caught fire with the realization of their lucky discovery.[49]

John Pemberton held onto the fledgling Coca-Cola Company until ill-health and insolvency forced him to sell his share of the business to Asa Griggs Candler, also a druggist and the producer of Botanic Blood Balm, a relatively successful patent medicine of the time. Candler immediately began to buy up shares of the Company from other partners until he finally owned the business outright in 1892. In 1888, however, a few shares short of his goal of sole proprietorship, he had moved what would ultimately become one of the largest and most successful corporations in the world out of the basement of Jacobs' drug store and into the basement of Asa G. Candler and Company with a single horse-drawn wagon.[50]

Asa Candler, some sons, several of his nephews, and Frank Robinson together marketed Coca-Cola enthusiastically, at first at home in Atlanta and eventually all over the nation and the world. They became innovative experts in the field of advertising as their novel ideas, such as free Coca-Cola coupons, won them both loyal consumers of Coca-Cola and the steadfast allegiance of the drugstore owners. Coupons would lure people into the drugstore to sample the drink, and while they waited at the fountain, they invariably thought of sundries to buy while they were in the store. Demand for syrup steadily increased year after year, forcing Candler, who had originally prepared Coca-Cola syrup in the same copper cauldron in which he mixed Botanic Blood Balm, to move his growing operation five different times to larger quarters.[51]

In 1916, at the annual meeting of The Coca-Cola Company, Asa G. Candler officially withdrew from active participation in the enterprise he had nurtured from a tiny basement plant into a multinational corporation enjoying great success in both fountain and bottling markets. Candler, who had just been elected Mayor of Atlanta and had yet to be inaugurated, said he needed to devote his full attention to his responsibilities as an elected official, and accordingly, he divided his majority shares among his wife and five chilren for Christmas in 1916, retaining only seven for himself.[52] His eldest son,

Charles Howard Candler, had succeeded to the presidency of The Coca-Cola Company in January of 1916, but the family saw this as only an interim office. They immediately began looking for a buyer and in 1918 formally put the Company up for sale.[53]

It was in 1919, three years after Asa Candler divided up The Coca-Cola Company, that the Woodruff syndicate approached the Candlers through the Chase National Bank and the Guaranty Trust Company of New York, offering them a $25,000,000 package for their shares in the Company—more than ten thousand times the amount Asa Candler had paid to purchase the Company thirty years earlier.[54] Ernest Woodruff had intentionally solicited the participation of the two New York banks, as he had reason to believe that Asa Candler would refuse to carry though with any deal in which Woodruff was involved. For reasons that are either unknown to or unspoken by any of the parties left living, Candler was vehemently opposed to doing business with Woodruff, so Woodruff very carefully stayed out of view during the banks' negotiations with the Candlers and conducted all of his own business with the banks in New York, keeping his participation in the deal so secret that, until it was announced to the public, his own sons knew nothing of the historic sale—and neither did Asa Candler.[55] Candler was not consulted at all by his children on the final terms of the deal and was so upset by the news of the transaction that he refused to attend the board meeting at which the sale was approved.[56]

The sale, announced on July 31, 1919, was closed several weeks later on August 23 in New York. The terms of the agreement were that the Candlers, in return for their majority shares, were to receive $10,000,000 in seven per cent cumulative first preferred stock in the new Delaware Coca-Cola Company that the syndicate planned to form to take advantage of that state's more advantageous corporate laws. The rest of their compensation would be in cash to be paid on or before September 1, roughly one week after closing the deal. The cash sum was to be somewhat less than $15,000,000, as the Company's unpaid taxes were to be borne by the sellers.[57]

George Woodruff was immensely pleased by the syndicate's acquisition of a controlling interest in The Coca-Cola Company, proud of his father's financial and organizational genius and believing without reservation that the Company was the best business around at the time.[58] Once the transaction was made public and Ernest Woodruff's involvement was brought to light, the press gave him complete credit for masterminding the whole deal, which they referred to at that time and for many decades thereafter as "the biggest financial affair of its kind ever put over in the South."[59] Although Ernest Woodruff went on the board of The Coca-Cola Company right away and George and Robert both would one day guide the affairs of the Company from the Board, there was no Woodruff family involvement in management immediately after the acquisition. Samuel Candler Dobbs, formerly the Company's vice president and general sales and advertising manager, was elected president by the new board on September 16,

Ernest Woodruff in about 1912.

1919, and The Coca-Cola Company continued its operation much in the same way it had for the previous thirty years.

After George Woodruff had worked as an engineer with Atlantic Ice & Coal for about a year, he moved on to a new position as the Georgia service manager for the White Motor Company, persuaded by his brother Robert to make what promised to be a career-advancing move. Robert had become involved with the White Motor Company through a circuitous route, beginning his business career at the General Pipe and Foundry Company in 1909 as an apprentice machinist. He was promoted after a year in that job to the position of assistant stock clerk with the General Fire Extinguisher Company, the parent of the Pipe and Foundry Company, and after a short time as a stock clerk, Robert was made a company salesman. His father, observing his developing expertise and beginning to forgive him for his defiance in leaving college, then gave him a job as purchasing agent for the recently reorganized Atlantic Ice & Coal Company, where his duties included purchasing all of the mules and wagons for delivering ice and coal to the company's customers.[60]

Because Atlantic Ice & Coal had shown a respectable profit in the years since its reorganization, its management and directors, including Ernest Woodruff, still felt that mule-drawn wagons were sound and reliable vehicles for carrying out the company's deliveries. Robert, however, had different ideas. With what was to become known as typical foresight and progressive business sense, he negotiated a deal with Walter White, the president of White Motor Company, to purchase a fleet of fifteen delivery trucks at or near manufacturing cost. Woodruff managed to convince White that it would be to the White Company's great advantage to display a fleet of delivery trucks in Atlanta, where autos and trucks were extremely scarce and there was a huge potential market for more efficient delivery systems. Although Ernest Woodruff reportedly almost collapsed when he heard of the purchase, the trucks were shortly performing the company's delivery services with great efficiency and savings, and Woodruff grudgingly pardoned what he had originally seen as his son's wild extravagance.[61]

Robert Woodruff's purchase of the fleet of White trucks accomplished more than merely overhauling and updating the Atlantic Ice & Coal Company's delivery service. When Woodruff discovered that a raise that he had been promised by the manager of the company had been vetoed by his father, he walked out of the plant and went straight to Walter White. White hired him immediately as a salesman for the White Motor Company, and by the time he convinced his younger brother George to join the company in 1920, he had risen to the position of Southeastern Regional Manager.[62]

For Robert, in building a strong White Company office in his home state, George's formal technical education and enthusiastic fascination with cars and motors were a formidable combination. Robert urged his brother to join the White Company, and George complied with his request, becoming an immense success in his work as state service manager. He was soon promoted to state sales manager, a timely and welcome advancement, as he and Irene were expecting their first child in early November of 1920.[63] Although George's traveling responsibilities were reduced considerably by his move to the White Company, he still spent about a week out of every month visiting White Company offices around the state. Irene had retired from traveling with George because of her pregnancy, and the two resumed their old habit of daily correspondence when they were separated, often reminiscing about their letters from their college days. "I love all your letters, whether they are short or long," Irene wrote on one occasion. "But the last one I received is the longest letter you have written me since I left school." Irene's letters were also filled with news and plans about their growing family. "If you don't hurry home you won't know me," Irene wrote to George as he called on the White Company branch in Macon in early April. "My looks are changing awfully fast." Feeling cramped in their small apartment on Ponce de Leon Avenue, Irene urged George to help her look for a house: " . . . if we *three* (doesn't that sound funny) can have our own little home . . . wouldn't it be wonderful?"[64]

First home of Mr. and Mrs. George W. Woodruff at 104 (later renumbered 1042) Oakdale Road. The lot for the house was bought and the home built in 1923 by Albert H. Bailey. It was sold on completion to the Woodruffs, and their second daughter, Mary Frances Woodruff, was born there.

Irene King Woodruff was born in George and Irene's Ponce de Leon Avenue apartment on November 8, 1918, to the collective joy of her parents, grandparents, aunts, and uncles. In early 1923, about a year and a half after little Irene's birth, George and Irene bought a small, one-story house at 104 Oakdale Road in Druid Hills, renumbered 1042 in 1926. The house had just been completed when George and Irene saw it while driving through the neighborhood, and with one daughter approaching the toddler stage and another child on the way, they thought the large yard would be ideal and arranged to close on the house as quickly as possible. Irene had just enough time to move from the apartment and begin to get settled in their new home before Mary Frances Woodruff, the second Woodruff daughter, was born on April 22, 1923.

The growing Woodruff family settled happily in their new home. George bought a cow to keep in the stable in the backyard for milk, and Irene hired a nurse, Lucy Harris, who would stay with the family until the last Woodruff daughter married and left home.[65] On September 30, 1925, the Woodruffs' third child, Jane, was born in her parents' house, which suddenly didn't seem as large as it had when they bought it.

George and Irene were naturally delighted by the birth of another daughter, but their tiny house seemed to shrink with the addition of another family member. Soon after Jane's birth and despite their affection for the little Oakdale Road house, George and Irene began looking seriously for larger quarters. In late 1925, they found a beautiful two-story red brick home at 212 Lullwater Road, the street adjacent to Oakdale Road, and moved the short distance to the new house as quickly as they could consummate the legal arrangements, planning to stay put for a long time.[66] What the George Woodruff family didn't know then, however, was that they would stay on Lullwater Road for only a short time before business intervened to take them farther from Atlanta than they had ever intended to go.

Ernest Woodruff, who had in 1923 prevailed upon his son Robert to leave his job as vice president and general manager of the White Motor Company to revive the ailing Coca-Cola Company, approached his son George in 1926 with a similar proposition. The Continental Gin Company, another of Ernest's reorganization projects, was in need of a young man in the management ranks with excellent technical training and qualifications, good experience, and a keen allegiance to ownership. George, sorry to leave Atlanta but thrilled with the opportunity, eagerly accepted his father's job offer, leaving the White Motor Company and packing his young family for the move to Birmingham, Alabama, headquarters of the Continental Gin Company.

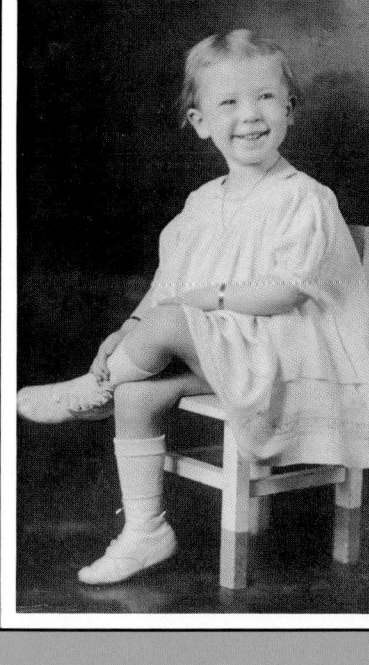

Irene King Woodruff, first child of George and Irene Woodruff, born in their first Atlanta apartment on Ponce de Leon Avenue near the old Sears building on November 8, 1920, shown here at age two. Irene married Alfred Benjamin Michael, Jr., on June 26, 1940.

Mary Frances Woodruff, taken in October of 1927 at age four. Frances was born on April 22, 1923, in the Woodruffs' home at 104 (now 1042) Oakdale Road, where the family lived until moving to 212 Lullwater Road. Frances married Robert Monroe Hallock of Jacksonville, Florida, on Saturday, August 28, 1943. They later divorced, and Frances retook the name Woodruff.

Jane Woodruff, in a carved squirrel chair, taken in October of 1927 at age two. Jane was born in the Woodruffs' home at 212 Lullwater Road on September 30, 1925, and married Richard W. King of Avon Park, Florida, on September 4, 1946. They later divorced, and Jane retook the Woodruff name.

The Clyde L. King family, Christmas 1924. From left to right, Irene King Woodruff is sitting on the lap of her father, George W. Woodruff, and next to her mother, Irene King Woodruff. Clara Belle Rushton King, Irene Woodruff's mother, holds George and Irene's second daughter, Frances. Clyde L. King, Irene's father, is seated to the right of Mrs. King, and Irene's younger sister Clara Belle and younger brother John follow. Clyde L. King, Jr., Irene's older brother, and his wife Frances Poole King are kneeling behind the group.

ENDNOTES

[1] Letter, George W. Woodruff to Irene Tift King, 8 January 1917.

[2] Letter, George W. Woodruff to Irene Tift King, 2 February 1917.

[3] Letter, George W. Woodruff to Irene Tift King, 8 January 1917.

Letter, George W. Woodruff to Irene Tift King, 5 February 1917.

[4] Letter, George W. Woodruff to Irene Tift King, 8 February 1917.

[5] Ibid.

[6] Letter, George W. Woodruff to Irene Tift King, 8 February 1917.

Letter, George W. Woodruff to Irene Tift King, 2 March 1917.

[7] Ibid.

[8] Letter, George W. Woodruff to Irene Tift King, 22 March 1917.

[9] Letter, George W. Woodruff to Irene Tift King, 24 March 1917.

[10] Letter, George W. Woodruff to Irene Tift King, 8 April 1917.

[11] Letter, George W. Woodruff to Irene Tift King, April 7, 1917.

[12] Ibid.

[13] Letter, George W. Woodruff to Irene Tift King, 7 April 1917.

Letter, George W. Woodruff to Irene Tift King, 16 April 1917.

Letter, George W. Woodruff to Irene Tift King, 10 April 1917.

Letter, George W. Woodruff to Irene Tift King, 16 April 1917.

[14] Letter, Irene Tift King to George W. Woodruff, 25 April 1917.

Letter, Irene Tift King to George W. Woodruff, 9 April 1917.

[15] Letter, Emily Winship Woodruff to George W. Woodruff, 4 May 1917.

Letter, Emily Winship Woodruff to George W. Woodruff, 1 May 1917.

[16] Letter, Emily Winship Woodruff to George W. Woodruff, 7 May 1917

[17] Letter, Emily Winship Woodruff to George W. Woodruff, 7 May 1917.

Letter, Emily Winship Woodruff to George W. Woodruff, 16 May 1917.

[18] Letter, George W. Woodruff to Irene Tift King, 13 April 1917.

[19] Letter, George W. Woodruff to Irene Tift King, 10 May 1917.

Letter, George W. Woodruff to Irene Tift King, 1 May 1917.

[20] Personal interview with George W. Woodruff, 31 December 1985.

[21] Personal interview with George W. Woodruff, 21 October 1986.

[22] Letter, George W. Woodruff to Irene Tift King, 9 March 1918.

[23] Letter, Irene Tift King to George W. Woodruff, 10 March 1918.

[24] Ibid.

Letter, Irene Tift King to George W. Woodruff, 6 April 1918.

[25] Letter, Irene Tift King to George W. Woodruff, 9 October 1917.

Letter, Irene Tift King to George W. Woodruff, 20 May 1917.

Personal interview with Vela Rocker, 5 September 1985.

[26] Letter, Irene Tift King to George W. Woodruff, 20 March 1918.

Personal interview with Jane Woodruff, 10 October 1986.

[27] Letter, Irene Tift King to George W. Woodruff, 10 March 1918.

[28] Letter, Irene Tift King to George W. Woodruff, 24 March 1918.

[29] Letter, Irene Tift King to George W. Woodruff, 10 March 1918.

Letter, Irene Tift King to George W. Woodruff, 20 March 1918.

[30] Letter, Irene Tift King to George W. Woodruff, 24 March 1918.

[31] Letter, George W. Woodruff to Irene Tift King, 4 April 1918.

Letter, George W. Woodruff to Irene Tift King, 8 April 1918.

[32] Letter, Irene Tift King to George W. Woodruff, 24 January 1917.

Letter, George W. Woodruff to Irene Tift King, 27 January 1917.

[33] Letter, Irene Tift King to George W. Woodruff, 2 February 1917.

[34] *The Atlanta Georgian,* "Miss Irene King Becomes Bride of George Woodruff," c. 18 April 1918, from Emily Winship Woodruff's personal scrapbook, in the possession of Jane Woodruff.

The Atlanta Constitution, "Wedding of Miss Irene Tift King and Mr. Woodruff Brilliant Event," 18 April 1918.

The Atlanta Constitution, "Mr. Geo. W. Woodruff Weds Miss Irene King," 18 April 1918.

Personal interview with George W. Woodruff, 31 December 1985.

The World Almanac and Book of Facts (1985), (New York: Newspaper Enterprise Association, Inc., 1985) 758.

[35] *The Atlanta Georgian,* "Wedding," c. 18 April 1918.

[36] Ibid.

[37] Letter, Irene Tift King to George W. Woodruff, 21 March 1918.

[38] Ibid.

Letter, Irene Tift King to George W. Woodruff, 25 March 1918, enclosing lease dated March 23, 1918.

[39] Lease between George W. Woodruff and Charles P. Ross dated March 23, 1918.

[40] Letter, George W. Woodruff to Irene Tift King, 22 July 1918.

[41] Personal interview with George W. Woodruff, 21 October 1986.

[42] Personal interview with George W. Woodruff, 31 December 1985.

The Blackmon Apartment Building at 371 Ponce de Leon was renumbered 563 in 1926.

[43] Personal interview with George W. Woodruff, 31 December 1985.

Coleman and Gurr, eds., *Georgia Biography,* 2:1083-1085.

Garrett, *Atlanta and Its Environs,* 2:413-15.

[44] Personal interviews with George W. Woodruff, 7 October 1986 and 21 October 1986.

[45] Personal interview with George W. Woodruff, 21 October 1986.

[46] Personal interview with George W. Woodruff, 31 December 1985.

[47] Watters, *Coca-Cola*, 45 ff.

[48] Ibid., 15.

[49] Ibid., 16.

[50] Ibid.

[51] Ibid., 32-33, 35, 37, 99.

[52] Ibid., 89.

Garrett, *Atlanta and Its Environs*, 2:699.

[53] Garrett, *Atlanta and Its Environs*, 2:699.

[54] Charles Elliott, *Mr. Anonymous: Robert W. Woodruff of Coca-Cola* (Atlanta: Cherokee Publishing Company, 1982) 116.

[55] Personal interview with George W. Woodruff, 26 May 1986, and 7 October 1986.

[56] Elliott, *Mr. Anonymous*, 116.

[57] *The Atlanta Journal*, 23 August 1919.

[58] Personal interview with George W. Woodruff, 20 May 1986.

[59] *The Atlanta Constitution*, n.d., clipping found in Emily Winship Woodruff's personal scrapbook, currently in the possession of Jane Woodruff.

[60] Personal interview with George W. Woodruff, 5 September 1985.

Elliott, *Mr. Anonymous*, 89-91.

[61] Ibid., 91.

[62] *The Genealogy of the Robert Winship Woodruff Family*, comp. Lucille Huffman (Atlanta: The Coca-Cola Company, 1973) 23.

[63] Personal interview with George W. Woodruff, 5 September 1985.

[64] Letter, Irene Tift King to George W. Woodruff, 9 May 1919.

Letter, Irene Tift King to George W. Woodruff, 8 April 1920.

Letter, Irene Tift King to George W. Woodruff, 11 April 1920.

[65] Personal interview with George W. Woodruff, 20 May 1986.

[66] Ibid.

Chapter Five

An Industrious Citizen

In 1926, when George Woodruff was offered the position of assistant to the president of the Continental Gin Company, Ernest Woodruff's syndicate had just acquired the business and the company itself had only been organized for twenty-seven years. Several of the companies that had merged to form Continental Gin in 1899, however, had far deeper roots, and their founders traced their manufacturing plans back to the late eighteenth century and the cotton gin's very first patents.

On March 14, 1794, a patent was issued to Eli Whitney for the world's first mechanical cotton gin, a device designed to separate cotton lint from its seed with rows of slender, revolving spikes. As the spikes in the gin turned, they passed through narrowly set metal ribs and pulled the cotton fibers away from the seeds, which were too large to pass through the small openings. The seeds would then drop into another compartment, and a revolving brush would clean the cotton fibers from the spikes. Whitney, a farm boy, Yale College graduate, and skilled mechanic from Westboro, Massachusetts, had built the gin while staying on a plantation in Savannah following his graduation from college. He worked for several weeks on the idea before unveiling and patenting his history-making invention, which was cranked by hand and could clean fifty pounds of cotton a day.[1]

A little more than two years after Eli Whitney had secured his patent, a man named Hogden Holmes patented a gin that substituted circular saws for the spikes in Whitney's gin and was the model for the ginning systems later made by the companies comprising the Continental Gin Company. The Holmes gin separated cotton fibers from the seed by means of circular saws mounted on a revolving cylinder, with the saws passing between closely set metal ribs that culled out the cotton seed. The real beauty of the Holmes gin, however, was the feed box on top of the gin frame, into which cotton could be dropped continuously by the gin's operators, eliminating any need to stop and start the gin with each batch of cotton. Because the Holmes gin could be operated without interruption, it could process much more cotton in a day, giving it a great advantage over the Whitney gin.[2]

Upon discovering the existence of the Holmes gin, Eli Whitney brought suit in federal court in Savannah in 1807 for patent infringement, and both inventors and a number of expert witnesses testified fully on the features of each machine. After hearing all of the evidence, Federal Court Judge William Johnson found Holmes's patent valid, holding that although Holmes had inarguably gotten the idea for his invention from the Whitney gin, his own execution of the concept was so far superior to Whitney's that it was patentable in its own right. The validity of Whitney's patent was also upheld, however, as the judge felt that Whitney's invention had supplied Holmes with the mechanical basis for his own work.[3]

Despite small and intermittent improvements, cotton gins stayed much as they were in 1796 until 1882, when Robert S. Munger, founder of the Munger Gin & Machine Company, was granted a series of patents on a ginning system that consisted of a battery of gins set up to work together, fed constantly by a suction device that pulled cotton onto a drag belt and carried it from a source of supply to the gins, the press, and the lint box. Munger enjoyed great success in marketing his invention until around 1899, when his patents began expiring. At that time, feeling that the future of his Munger Gin & Machine Company would be more secure as a component of a larger enterprise, Munger negotiated a merger with the Eagle Gin Company, the Smith & Sons Gin Company, the Pratt Gin Company, the Munger-Northington-Pratt Gin Company, and the Winship Machine Company, George Woodruff's grandfather Winship's concern. The merged firm, known as the Continental Gin Company, carried on its business under central management in Prattville, Alabama, from the separate plants of the original companies. Although the Continental Gin Company manufactured the Eagle Plain Gin, the Pratt Double Rib Huller Gin, and the Munger system for a short time, efforts were soon consolidated in the production of the latter two, which remained the company's staple machinery for many years.[4]

When George Woodruff arrived in Birmingham in 1926 to begin his new job as assistant to the president of the Continental Gin Company, he was thirty-one years old and had never seen a cotton gin before, but his lack of exposure did not daunt him. Because of the years he had spent at Tech High, Georgia Tech, and M.I.T., Woodruff was confident in his ability to learn the business, although he did say later that without his extensive prior training, he would never have understood the operation of the machine itself or its manufacturing process, regardless of any confidence or willingness to learn.[5] In addition to his impressive academic background and experience in technological areas, Woodruff also had the advantage of an able and interested instructor in the fine points of his new job. Thomas Elliott, Continental Gin's president, had been guiding the company's affairs since the time that the six gin concerns were merged in 1899, and he saw Woodruff's apprenticeship as a welcome opportunity to begin looking toward a long-awaited retirement.[6]

As Woodruff applied himself to his new job with great energy and enthusiasm, he fully realized that his position at the Gin Company was the ideal combination of all his interests and skills. He learned the business quickly and enjoyed the wood, tin, machine, and foundry shop processes that went into assembling the cotton gins as much as he did the mechanical operation of the final product. Woodruff had also become very interested in business during the time he spent with his father in New York while he was in college, and his position with the Continental Gin Company allowed him the opportunity to exercise his skills in that area. In addition to his engineering responsibilities in the area of new designs and machine overhauls, his job required that he oversee all facets of the company's business operation, including finances, stock performance, and plans for future growth.[7]

Within four years of Woodruff's arrival in Birmingham, Thomas Elliott, confident that the business was in good hands, gratefully resigned from his position as president of Continental Gin to go into partial retirement, continuing to serve the company on a part-time basis as a consulting engineer. The board of directors, pleased by the increase in the dividend rate on common stock from four to five dollars per share and by financial reports that showed 1929 to have been one of the most prosperous years in the company's history, credited Woodruff's efforts with much of that success and elected him to succeed Elliott as president of the company in February of 1930. After four years as president of Continental Gin, Woodruff was elevated to chairman of the board.[8]

Woodruff's involvement in all of the facets of the company's operation demanded long hours, and his days began early in Birmingham. He started out with breakfast at the house with Irene and the girls and moved next to Continental Gin's plant, where he would start his work day by presiding over a meeting of the department heads, leading a discussion of financial, design, marketing, and production reports for fifteen minutes to an hour before adjourning the assemblage to attend to the day's tasks. He would then work at his desk for several hours before lunch in the plant cafeteria, where all of the plant's management, engineers, shop foremen, and employees would eat together and discuss Continental Gin's business.

In the afternoons, Woodruff would take a tour of the plant, which occupied about ten acres of land on the outskirts of Birmingham and consisted of a big machine shop, a wood shop, a tin shop, a foundry, and a warehouse in addition to the two-story main office building. Each shop occupied its own separate building on the plant grounds, and although they were close together, the sheer size of the individual structures made Woodruff's afternoon tour a grand expedition. Stopping to talk with each of the foremen and occasionally

The Continental Gin Company, Birmingham, Alabama, in July of 1939. George W. Woodruff was named assistant to the president of the company in 1926, president in 1930, chairman of the board in 1934, and chairman of the executive committee in 1955. In 1959, the Woodruff interests sold the Continental Gin Company, and the purchaser closed the Birmingham plant, moving the company's operations to the plant in Prattville, Alabama.

rolling up his sleeves to demonstrate a machining technique to a shopworker, he would spend approximately two hours touring the plant before returning to his office for more desk work.[9]

The Continental Gin Company, the world's premier manufacturer of ginning equipment, produced and assembled all of the component parts for cotton gins. Also, because the equipment necessary to manufacture gins lent itself naturally to the production of conveyers, the company soon began making conveying equipment for moving cotton from machine to machine in multiple gin setups.[10] Once Continental Gin had ventured into that market, the product line expanded still further as the company began receiving requests for custom work. George Morgan, one of Continental Gin's engineers, had the job of designing conveyers to accommodate individual customers' needs for specialized product moving equipment, one particularly ingenious example of which transported coal from the entrance of a mine across a ravine, around a bend, and over quite a distance of flat land to reach a processing area, where it was then dumped into bins to be held for sorting.[11]

Throughout his long career at Continental Gin, some of Woodruff's chief sources of pride in his work were the company's business success, creativity, and continued superiority in mechanical design. He derived great pleasure from any technological innovation and, he later remembered, some of his finest moments at the helm of his company were those when Continental Gin announced an improved design for a gin or one of its integral parts. Through the course of his career with the company, Woodruff enjoyed many such fine moments, as the company made huge strides in modernization under his leadership. When he joined Continental Gin as assistant to the president in 1926, the gins the company manufactured were, aside from their iron legs, made entirely of wood. Soon after his arrival, however, Woodruff began directing the company in a systematic process of changing over the various wood components, which even included the spikes, ribs, and roll boxes at that time, to steel, until finally, after a period of about forty years, the gins, baling presses, and hull extracters were wholly made of steel.[12]

Continental Gin Company lint removal machines.

Although the company continued for a period of time to operate from the plants of each of the concerns that had merged in 1899 to form Continental Gin, those outlying factories were gradually closed due to the combined effects of a reduced demand for cotton resulting from the advent of synthetic fabric and a great improvement in Continental Gin's facilities in Birmingham that enabled the company to meet all production needs there. The factory in Atlanta, the Winship family's concern, closed around 1943, while production in Dallas, Texas, and Prattville, Alabama, continued for a period thereafter. The company kept its sales office and parts depot in Memphis open as well.[13]

With relatively few Continental Gin plants and sales offices to serve the needs of cotton producers all over the South and West, George Woodruff frequently found himself traveling to present the merits of Continental Gin's equipment to potential customers. Even the smallest ginning operation, usually a single plantation, would require two gins to make cotton processing economically feasible, and two gins were a purchase which even in the twenties and thirties represented an outlay of thirty to forty thousand dollars. Commercial ginners employed even more machinery, normally buying a set of four to six gins to work concurrently in a production unit known in the cotton business as an outfit, and both small plantations and commercial ginners were also likely to need additional equipment such as hull-extractors, cleaning machinery, and baling presses to pack the cotton once it was ginned. Baled cotton was sold to cotton mills, and cotton mills spun the raw cotton into yarn and wove the yarn into cloth, which was then sold to clothing manufacturers.[14]

The sheer magnitude in dollars of each sale dictated Woodruff's presence on selling trips, and, with the superintendent of the Birmingham plant accompanying him, he would zig-zag by car through the Carolinas, Georgia, Alabama, Texas, Arkansas, Florida, Louisiana, Mississippi, Missouri, New Mexico, Oklahoma, Tennessee, and anywhere else cotton was grown or processed, calling on ginners and farmers to sell them Continental Gin's wares. Woodruff's sales technique, simple but imminently successful, consisted of describing to

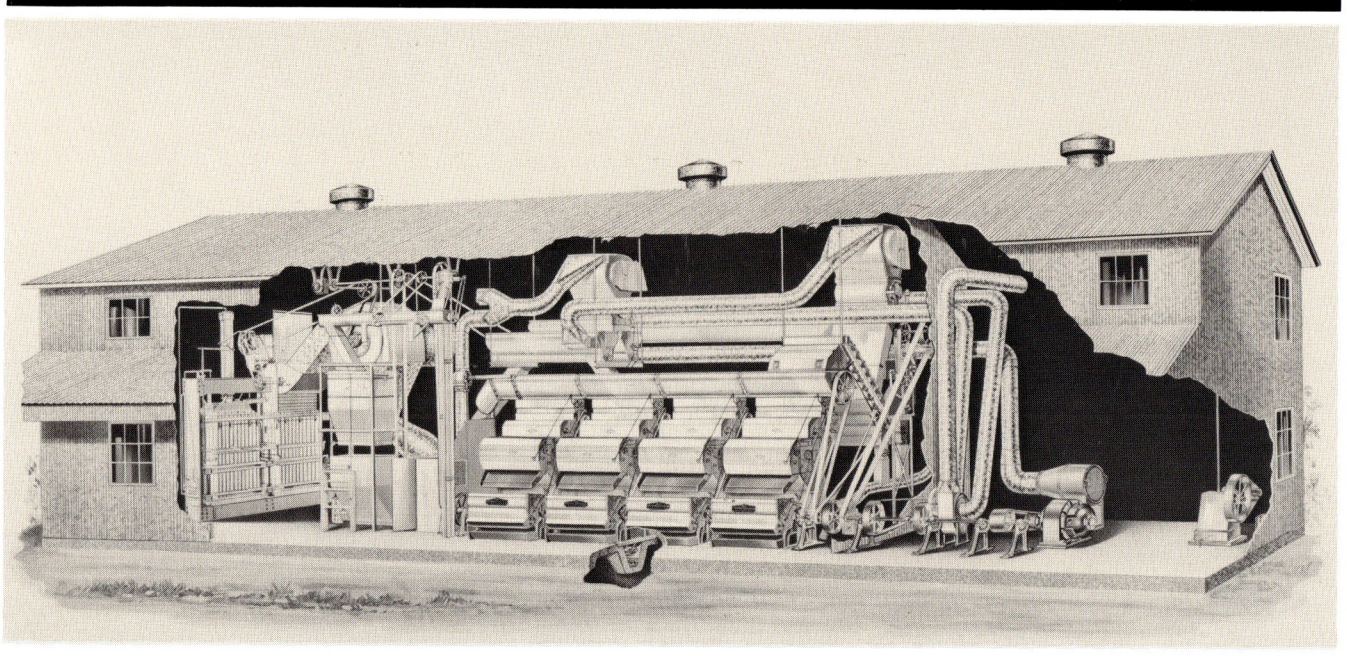

Complete Continental Gin Company cotton ginning system in Birmingham.

the ginners the operation of the equipment and the features of that operation that distinguished Continental Gin's machines from those of its competitors, the Lummus Gin Company of Columbus, Georgia, and the Murray Gin Company of Dallas, Texas. While he later admitted that he did on occasion lose a sale to one of those companies, his success rate was high, and if he ever felt that the Continental Gin line was not superior to its competitors, he and his engineers would study the rival's machines until they discovered a way to similarly enhance the capabilities of the Continental Gin line.[15]

It was not long after the young Woodruff family moved to Birmingham that they became completely acclimated to their new surroundings and involved in the life of the community. George Woodruff joined the Birmingham Country Club and the Robuck Golf Club shortly after his arrival in the city, and he was soon after invited to become a member of both the Birmingham Rotary Club and the board of directors of the Birmingham Trust and National Bank. Upon accepting the Continental Gin Company's offer of a job, Woodruff had sold the family's new house on Lullwater Road in Atlanta and bought a large home set on a spacious, tree-filled lot at 4316 Ninth Court South in Birmingham. The yard held a small barn with stalls for the family's cow and the Mexican burro that the girls' grandfather King had given them before they left Atlanta, and when Woodruff built the children a playhouse not far from the barn and hung a swing from one of the trees behind the house, he secured his yard's reputation as one of the best playgrounds in the neighborhood, and his daughters never lacked for companions. Even Woodruff enjoyed riding the burro around the yard and driveway for the entertainment of his children and their friends, and Irene captured the amusing sight of her husband astride the short, squat animal in a series of home movies taken while the family was in Birmingham.[16]

George W. Woodruff, taken about 1932, several years after he was named president of the Continental Gin Company.

Irene and George Woodruff in about 1927 in Birmingham, Alabama, where the family moved in 1926 upon George Woodruff's assumption of the position of assistant to the president of the Continental Gin Company.

Along with the other children in the neighborhood, the two older Woodruff girls attended Avondale Grammar School, a coed public school near their home on Ninth Court South, where Frances participated in plays and pageants, while Irene became interested in piano and began lessons with a private teacher. Jane, only a year old at the time of the family's move to Birmingham, spent her days at home with her mother and nurse, Lucy Harris, known to the children as Mammy.[17] Although Woodruff often did bring work home in the evenings, he also spent a great deal of time with his wife and children, and Sundays especially were saved for family outings. Following the tradition of the Ernest Woodruff family when George was growing up, George, Irene, little Irene, Frances, and Jane would often go for long rides in the car on Sunday afternoons, traveling to various points of interest around the city. Red Mountain was a favorite destination while the family was in Birmingham, and the children very much enjoyed going to the Grant Park Zoo when visiting grandparents in Atlanta.[18] Sometimes their trips were longer, and Jane Woodruff remembered one extended vacation in particular when the Woodruffs combined business with pleasure on a long trip out West as the family accompanied Woodruff on a selling trip for the Continental Gin Company.[19]

Because the young Woodruff family saw the senior Woodruffs and the Kings only infrequently, vacation time that George was able to take from the Continental Gin Company was usually spent in Atlanta. The family would drive to Atlanta for whatever time was avail-

George and Irene Woodruff with daughters Jane (in Mrs. Woodruff's arms), Irene (left), and Frances (right), at home at 4316 Ninth Court South, Birmingham, Alabama on May 28, 1926.

able and divide their stay equally between the grandparents' homes.[20] As Jane Woodruff later remembered, the two sets of grandparents and the atmosphere in each of their homes were vastly different, and the children gained a new understanding of their own parents' natures by watching them interact with the Woodruffs and the Kings. The environment in the Woodruff household was stern and austere, governed by habit and an inflexible adhesion to an unspoken but implicitly understood code of behavior and system of values. Emily and Ernest, whom the children knew as Monie and Pa, were very restrained in their demeanor, affording the time for a brief pat on the head or hug for their grandchildren, but when the moment was over, the children understood that they were to disappear quickly and play quietly elsewhere. Ernest, always imposing and serious, was completely and continuously engrossed in matters of business and expected his home to operate as smoothly and efficiently as did the Trust Company of Georgia or Atlantic Ice & Coal. Emily, as the elegant and impenetrably dignified chief executive officer of their home, made certain that Ernest's expectations were not upset; loud noises, emotional outbursts, and fingerprints on the wallpaper were not tolerated.[21]

Clara Belle and Clyde King in the 1930s.

At the King home on Ponce de Leon Avenue, however, the atmosphere was decidedly different. Irene's mother, the children's grandmother King, was warm and energetic, much like Irene herself. Perhaps because the Kings still had a child at home, Irene's youngest brother John, they were tolerant, even indulgent, towards the children's sometimes boisterous enthusiasm. Where Monie was an adored but aloof image, Grandmother King was a sympathetic lap and encouraging voice, and the children looked forward to the time they spent with her. Another attraction at the King household was Irene's brother John who was only eight years older than little Irene Woodruff, and the Woodruff children enjoyed their young uncle as much as they did his toys. John had a goat cart similar to the one George Woodruff had enjoyed as a child in Inman Park, as well as a pony, and the four children played happily together.[22]

George and Irene Woodruff and their children lived contentedly in Birmingham for about seven years before they began considering a

The Woodruff children in John King's goat cart, which was much like the one their father enjoyed as a child. Taken in January of 1928, the picture shows Catherine McKenzie, Lillian Faulkes, and Irene standing from left to right, and Jane, Mary Alice (a friend), and Frances in the cart. The man leading the goat is identified as "Preacher," and was most likely a retainer in the Clyde King home.

move to Daytona Beach, Florida. Jane had been suffering from nagging childhood illnesses in Birmingham, and, as the fame and profitability of The Coca-Cola Company grew and George Woodruff became well known for his own business success, Irene and George grew increasingly conscious of their own and their children's vulnerability to kidnapping and extortion. Nineteen thirty-two had seen the kidnapping of Charles A. Lindbergh's infant son end in tragedy, and when the Hamm, Urschel, and Hart kidnappings followed in 1933, the Woodruffs decided that they would prefer to live and raise their children in a smaller, safer town and a more temperate climate.[23] It is said that in the heat of the kidnapping scare of the thirties Emily Woodruff was asked whether she feared that her husband Ernest, who was known for his somewhat irascible disposition, would fall prey to such an attack. "Goodness, no," Emily responded lightly. "If anyone ever did take Ernest, they certainly wouldn't keep him very long."[24] George Woodruff was not so cavalier about his own immediate family, however, so in about 1933, he rented a luxurious home at 1400 South Peninsula Drive in Daytona with an option to buy, and he and Irene packed up their household, comprised then of little Irene, Frances, and Jane, then twelve, ten, and nine years old respectively, Mammy, and Julia Jackson, the cook, and moved from Alabama to Florida.[25]

Side view of the Woodruffs' home at 1400 South Peninsula Drive in Daytona Beach, Florida. The house fronted on the Halifax River, where George Woodruff kept his boat Monie. *The house, yard, and swimming pool were the sites of numerous gala social events, including elegant garden parties for the Palmetto Club of Daytona Beach, as well as the wedding of the eldest daughter, Irene.*

George W. Woodruff on his boat Monie *in Daytona Beach, Florida. the* Monie *was named for Woodruff's mother, Emily Winship Woodruff.*

The Woodruffs' new house at 1400 South Peninsula Drive fronted on the Halifax River and had been built and owned by the Cheek family of Daytona in the early 1900s. The large front yard contained a picturesque swimming pool and a tennis court, and Woodruff kept his well-loved and constantly used twin-engine Chris Craft cruiser, named *Monie* after his mother and his grandmother Winship, docked at the edge of the river. The house itself had three stories, with five bedrooms, as many baths, extensive servants' quarters, and a separate wing for laundry and ironing. While Irene was pleased with the graciousness and beauty of her large new home, George Woodruff focused on the merits of the spacious four-car garage and the convenient access to his boat, a hobby he took up upon the family's move to Daytona. Daytona also offered the perfect climate for year-round golf, Woodruff's favorite pastime, and he immediately took advantage of the accommodating weather by joining the Daytona Country Club, the Seabreeze Country Club, and the Gulf Stream Country Club in Delray Beach, Florida.[27]

The three girls also found their new town well-suited to their interests and activities. Irene and George enrolled them in Daytona's

Graham-Eckes School, and they quickly became active in the pursuits they had enjoyed in Birmingham. Jane began and little Irene continued piano lessons, and the family's home movies and photographs capture the many elaborate outdoor recitals that Irene hosted for her daughters' music school on the lawn at the bank of the Halifax River. The large lawn was also the frequent site of elegant garden parties for Daytona Beach's Palmetto Garden Club, and the festivities at any one such party were likely to include an outdoor fashion show, a swimming and diving exhibition, dance and vocal recitals, and a fortune-telling booth. At one particularly lavish function, a local high school glee club provided non-stop musical entertainment from two yachts anchored at the riverbank.[28] Jane Woodruff also entertained her young friends on the locally famous lawn, although her choice of activities was considerably more suited to her age and interests. Starting a coed football team with her father's encouragement soon after the family's move to Florida, Jane spent many Saturdays in enthusiastic athletic skirmishes with her friends as George Woodruff looked on with amusement, occasionally tossing a ball to the young players. Irene provided hamburgers after the game.[29]

Throughout the time that the Woodruffs lived in Daytona Beach, one of the family's favorite vacation spots was the small mountain village of Highlands in North Carolina. The Woodruffs first started spending time in Highlands while they were living in Birmingham in the early 1930s, traveling up into the mountains by car in the summers to stay in the small cottages at the Highlands Country Club. In 1940, Woodruff hired architect Henry Jordan to design a permanent vacation home for the family in Highlands, and Woodruff was active in suggesting different features he felt would enhance his family's enjoyment of the time they spent there. Most important, Woodruff told Jordan, was a large central living room, where family and guests could gather for talking, card games, or just knitting or

From left to right, Irene King Woodruff, Mary Frances Woodruff, and Jane Woodruff in the yard at 1400 South Peninsula Drive in Daytona Beach, Florida. Taken in 1938, the photograph shows Irene at age 18, Frances at age fifteen, and Jane at age thirteen.

reading. He also wanted to be certain that there was sufficient bedroom space for guests, the children, and later, the children's families, to come and stay at any time without feeling that they were crowding Irene and George or each other. To accommodate Woodruff's request, Jordan designed a large interior balcony that circled above the living room, with the second floor bedrooms opening out into the open space. The house also had an expansive front porch, where the family and their guests would sit to enjoy the cool air and view of the mountains.[30]

The Woodruffs stayed in the new house, named Ruffwood, for the first time in 1941 and immediately felt at home. Always cool in the heat of the summer and a quiet escape from the demands of the city, Ruffwood became the Woodruffs' favorite place to spend time. The whole family looked forward each summer to their stay in Highlands, and family servants saw their time at Ruffwood as a paid vacation, as the general tranquility and informality made working there a peaceful respite from normal routine.[31] The Woodruffs also commonly invited friends to come up from Atlanta to stay with them in Highlands, where the men would play golf at the Highlands Country Club during the day, nap upon their return to Ruffwood in the afternoon, and start a game of gin rummy or, less frequently, poker at night. While the men were otherwise engaged, Irene would entertain the wives with sightseeing, conversation, and needlework.[32] Irene Woodruff was known among her friends for her devotion to her husband, and some of the most profound examples of that dedication were witnessed by friends in Highlands. While George and the other three members of his invited foursome slept or ate breakfast, Irene would be spotted driving to the Highlands Country Club, which did not allow members to make their tee times over the telephone, to make George's tee time for him.[33]

Front view of the Woodruffs' summer home "Ruffwood" in Highlands, North Carolina. George Woodruff began construction on the home in 1940, and the family began spending summers at "Ruffwood" in 1941. The Woodruff family had been spending time in Highlands prior to building their summer home, staying in the small cottages available for rent at the Highlands Country Club. After they built their home, Highlands was a favorite gathering spot for them and their children, grandchildren, and friends, who came to Highlands to enjoy each other's company and the family's favorite activities—golf and gin rummy. Woodruff later gave "Ruffwood" to his youngest daughter, Jane.

While George Woodruff often said that the Highlands Country Club course, because of its ease and beauty, was his favorite place to play golf, he loved the game itself more than any particular course and played avidly whenever he had the opportunity. He started playing on his father's membership at the Druid Hills Golf Club when he was twelve years old, as golf was one of the few pleasures that the rigid Ernest permitted himself to enjoy, and he encouraged his young sons to adopt the pastime as well. After learning to play golf at Druid Hills, George Woodruff joined the East Lake Country Club and signed on to take lessons from Stewart Maiden, the same pro who was then teaching the famous Bobby Jones to play. Through his connection with Maiden and the club, he began playing golf with Jones and con-

George and Irene Woodruff at "Ruffwood" in Highlands around 1942.

tinued to play with him about once a month through the remainder of Jones' active golf career, although, he once said wryly, he never beat him.[34]

    Woodruff was a member of many golf clubs throughout his life and kept a bag of clubs at every one of them. He joined the Druid Hills Golf Club as a high school student, and he later and at various times was a member of the East Lake Country Club, the Capital City Club, the Birmingham Country Club and the Robuck Golf Club in Birmingham, the Sea Breeze Country Club and the Daytona Country Club in Daytona Beach, the Gulf Stream Club in Delray Beach, the Highlands Country Club, the Wild Cat Cliffs Club near Highlands, and the Peachtree Golf Club, where he was one of the first members to own a golf cart. One of his favorite courses, however, was the Augusta National Golf Club, where Bobby Jones had sponsored Woodruff for membership.[35] Woodruff's love of the golf was legendary. He saw the combination of a club, ball, and green as the ideal forum for testing and demonstrating his skill and played as often as he could, at least twice a week on Wednesdays and Saturdays. After his retirement from the Continental Gin Company, he formed a regular Sunday foursome as well. Johnnie Westmoreland, Hugh Carter, Bob White, and Ralph Paris played with Woodruff on Sundays, and he also frequently took them with him to play at Augusta National and

Highlands. Other frequent companions were Charlie Yates, Julian Harrison, Billy Wardlaw, Bill Parker, Alfred Boylston, long-time Trust Company friend and associate John A. Sibley, and retired Army General Clark L. Ruffner, the latter two of whom were favored guests in Highlands. When companions or time for a full game were lacking, Woodruff would go out in the side yard at the house to practice putting.[36]

Despite Woodruff's extreme modesty about his golfing abilities, he was well known among his friends and acquaintances for his putting, although he frequently and humbly insisted that he really didn't putt very well at all. Donn Gaebelein, president of The Westminster Schools, kindly contradicted Woodruff on that point and recalled meeting him for the first time on a golf course after former Mayor Ivan Allen, Jr. had asked Gaebelein to join a Rotary foursome on Rotary Outing Day with Allen, George Woodruff, and Ed Smith. Having assumed the presidency of Westminster only several years before, Gaebelein remembered being somewhat in awe of the situation, both because of his older companions' standing in the community and their well-known golfing abilities, as Gaebelein, by his own estimation, had never putted very well. The foursome played four or five holes, and Gaebelein became increasingly nervous as he realized that Woodruff had been watching him three-putt each one. Finally, as Gaebelein tells the story, Woodruff could not stand to watch him putt another time. He strode over to where Gaebelein was standing, thrust out his open hand and said authoritatively and succinctly, "Here." Gaebelein handed over the putter wordlessly, and Woodruff took it, bending at the same time to pick up Gaebelein's ball. Setting down the ball about thirty feet from the hole, he turned back to the by then embarrassed and bemused Gaebelein and called, "Watch." He swung at the ball and knocked it into the distant hole as Gaebelein looked on. He then picked up another ball, placed it in front of him and, telling Gaebelein to stroke *through* the ball, hit the second ball cleanly into the hole. Gaebelein later said that his initial embarrassment at the older man's scrutiny of his golf game evaporated instantly as he recognized the kindness and interest behind Woodruff's gesture. Woodruff, said Gaebelein, put out a bridge of friendship that spanned the many years difference in their ages and formed the basis of a cordial relationship that lasted for the rest of Woodruff's life.[37]

While Woodruff said that the lowest golf score he ever had was about a seventy-five on the Peachtree course, he remembered the best game he ever played as one at the Country Club of Naples in Florida in 1968, where his score was far higher than seventy-five, but he shot a hole-in-one. He remembered playing rather well in a foursome made up of Ed Callaham, Perry Crawford, and Phil Sowersby until he

George Woodruff with the other members of his golf foursome, Ed Callaham, Perry Crawford, and Phil Sowersby, after shooting a hole-in-one at the Country Club of Naples in Florida in 1968.

made the historic shot over a seemingly yawning lake into the 165-yard sixth hole. After the shot, however, he was too excited to concentrate, and his score climbed rapidly.[38]

Although Woodruff's first interest in Highlands was the golf course, he had many other involvements in the community and the region in addition to the country club. He gave generously to help support and expand the Highlands-Cashiers Hospital and also guided the management of the hospital for many years as a trustee. More recently, Woodruff gave funds to construct a community center in Highlands to provide local residents with a place to meet and hold athletic events. The facility, which provided Highlands with a gymnasium, exercise rooms, and a kitchen, was named the George and Irene Woodruff Community Center and opened in 1985.[39]

Another long-time interest in the Highlands area was the Rabun Gap-Nacoochee School, a private school approximately fourteen miles from Ruffwood, which the Woodruff family began supporting in about 1903. At that time, Dr. Andrew Ritchie, a Rabun County native who was trying to raise funds to build a school for children of the Rabun Gap region, went from door to door in Inman Park seeking donations. Emily Woodruff felt that the establishment of an institution to help alleviate poverty, illiteracy, and isolation among the mountain children was a good cause and gave Dr. Ritchie small sums out of her grocery money to help him build the Rabun Gap Industrial School.[40] Dr. Ritchie's plan for the school was that the students, who were almost as a rule too poor to attend a conventional private school, would be able during their free time to perform much of the work a non-faculty staff would normally carry out, saving the school the cost of paying such a staff and thereby helping to fund the students' tuition.[41]

Dr. Ritchie's plan was a success, and Emily Woodruff continued to give to the Rabun Gap School from her grocery money over a number of years until Dr. Ritchie, in need of a large infusion of capital for his planned Farm Family Program, approached Ernest Woodruff in 1920 with a request for more substantial support. Ernest graciously complied and encouraged friends and business associates from Atlanta, New York, and Boston to give to the program that would teach whole families to farm in an economically and agriculturally enlightened way.[42] Ernest and Emily Woodruff maintained their increased level of giving after their 1920 donation, and Ernest was one of the incorporating trustees of the Rabun Gap-Nacoochee School, formed in 1928 through the merger of Rabun Gap Industrial School and Nacoochee Institute, a school that had been chartered near Helen, Georgia, around the same time as the Rabun Gap Industrial School was founded. Each institution had suffered a disastrous fire in 1926, and as they were similarly chartered to help lift the mountain children from poverty and isolation, a merger seemed a wise course for the consolidation of the schools' financial needs and resources.

George Woodruff, although aware of the school's existence from the time his mother first began giving small sums to Dr. Ritchie, first took an active role in the affairs of Rabun Gap-Nacoochee in 1937 during a campaign to raise funds for an endowment for the school. George, Robert, and Ernest Woodruff each individually pledged a significant sum to the endowment fund, and that same year, at his father's request, George also took over Ernest's place on the school's board of trustees.[43] In 1940, after the death of J. B. Campbell, George Woodruff was elected to succeed Campbell as chairman of the board of trustees.[44]

George Woodruff guided Rabun Gap-Nacoochee School in his official capacity as a trustee for thirty-three years, finally retiring in 1974 after the Presbyterian Synod of Georgia, which oversees the school, enacted the provision in 1963 that no individual could serve on the board of any one of the Synod's institutions more than three consecutive three-year terms. During his long tenure as a trustee, Woodruff was generous in his gifts to the school as well as diligent in his leadership. He advised the school in major improvements to its physical plant, including the modernization of the dormitories' heating systems and the school's water system and the construction of the George W. Woodruff Dormitory, the Emily Winship Woodruff Administration Building, and the school's chapel, which was also dedicated to the memory of Emily and Ernest Woodruff.[45]

After he stepped down from the board of trustees, George Woodruff continued to take an active interest in the school, visiting the campus frequently when he was on his way to Highlands and advising the school's administration on various matters of concern. Dr. Karl Anderson, president of Rabun Gap-Nacoochee School from 1956 until his retirement in 1984, remembered George Woodruff as an ideal leader, particularly for a school with a curriculum grounded in practical application. While Anderson was warmed by Woodruff's graciousness and friendliness, he most admired his leadership qualities, calling him "methodical, thorough, decisive, and strong."[46] During times of conflict among the trustees, Woodruff could be counted upon to marshall the strengths of various board members' opinions and reach a solution satisfactory to the whole board and to the benefit of the school. In 1967, when the board of trustees was struggling with the issue of integration, Woodruff, who was absolutely unshakable in his beliefs once he had thoroughly considered a problem and reached a decision, moved in a positive way to bring Rabun Gap-Nacoochee School to a progressive stance on integration, and the board of trustees willingly followed his confident lead.[47] Woodruff also continued to support the school financially, and in 1976, the Irene King Woodruff Hall for girls was dedicated on the Rabun Gap-Nacoochee campus in honor forty years of interest by both Irene and George. George's interest in the school continued until his death, and Rabun Gap-Nacoochee bears significant evidence of the contributions he made throughout his lifetime.

After Ruffwood was completed in 1941, the Woodruff family began the practice of moving up to Highlands officially in May every year, and aside from necessary business and social trips to Atlanta and elsewhere, they would stay until the house was closed for the winter in October. Little Irene, Frances, and Jane would also spend their entire summers in Highlands, aside from random weeks spent at a camp for girls in Sapphire, North Carolina. As the Woodruff daughters reached their teenage years, they found, in addition to the peaceful atmosphere and the cool weather, a number of social interests among the people in the Highlands community. Around 1936, when the family was still staying in rented cottages at the Highlands Country Club, the girls met Bobby and Dick King, sons of the family that owned the King's Inn in Highlands. The two King boys were also friends with Alfred Michael, whose family was in the citrus business in Wabasso, Florida, and owned a farmhouse in Highlands where they spent their summers. Dick King and Alfred Michael attended the University of Florida together, and one of their Alpha Tau Omega fraternity brothers there, Bob Hallock, began to accompany Dick and Alfred on their visits to the Woodruff daughters. Alfred and Bob both had their pilot's licenses, so in the winters, when the boys were at school in Gainesville and the Woodruffs were at home in Daytona Beach, Alfred, Bob, and Dick would fly to Daytona, landing on the beach near the house on South Peninsula Drive, to visit the sisters.[48]

After her graduation from Daytona's Graham-Eckes School, Irene left home to attend the King-Smith Studio School, a finishing school for artists in Washington, D.C.[49] Following graduation from the Studio School, she was a debutante in Orlando, Florida, for a year before marrying Alfred B. Michael, whom she had met up at Highlands and dated steadily through school. Irene and Alfred were married in one of the last great lawn extravaganzas of the Woodruff family's residence at 1400 South Peninsula Drive, leaving their wedding reception for their honeymoon on board George Woodruff's cruiser, *Monie*, from the lawn in front of the house.[50]

In the mid 1940s, not long after Irene and Alfred's wedding, George and Irene Woodruff sold the house at 1400 South Peninsula Drive to return to live permanently in Atlanta. The family had been commuting between Daytona and Atlanta since 1937, when Emily Woodruff, and shortly after, Clara Belle King became ill. Emily died in August of 1939 at the age of seventy-two, and Clara Belle's death at the age of sixty-two followed in December of the same year. When Ernest Woodruff and Clyde King then began to weaken rapidly, George and Irene, having by that point spent long periods of time living away from home at the Biltmore Hotel on West Peachtree Street and in the senior Woodruffs' house in Druid Hills, decided for a number of reasons that they would prefer to live in Atlanta again on a permanent basis. They put the Daytona house on the market, and, realizing both that the onset of World War II had created a great demand for patrol boats and that a large cruiser would be of limited use

You are invited to the dedication of two residence halls Irene King Woodruff Hall and Karl Anderson Hall at Rabun Gap-Nacoochee School 12:30 p.m. Friday, September 17, 1976

Invitation to the dedication of two residence halls at Rabun Gap-Nacoochee School.

in land-locked Atlanta, sold the *Monie* to the government for one dollar.[51]

With their return to their native city in the early 1940s, the George Woodruff family joined a small throng of former Atlantans coming back home. The mid-1940s had witnessed the end of the enforcement of an unreasonably oppressive Georgia intangibles tax that had effectively kept the whole Woodruff family, along with many other wealthy Atlantans, away from the city for close to a decade. Enforcement of the inhospitable tax had come about in 1935, when the State of Georgia had decided to revive an ancient but long ignored intangibles tax law grounded on a provision in the state Constitution of 1877, which required that intangible property—stock, bonds, notes, and evidence of indebtedness—would be assessed for ad valorem taxation at rates and valuations uniform to those applicable to tangible personal property.[52] The law's reemergence from obscurity quickly rendered The Coca-Cola-Company's stockholders' continued residence in Georgia impossible, as the tax, already high, provided for an even higher rate on stock held in foreign corporations, and the Company had been reincorporated in Delaware when Ernest Woodruff's consortium bought out the Candlers in 1919. Although dormant for years and previously honored only in the breach, then Governor Eugene Talmadge saw the enforcement of the old law as the quickest and easiest way to raise much-needed dollars for the Depression-haunted state. The Georgia General Assembly was rurally dominated, and there was very little intangible wealth in Georgia's rural communities. Consequently, the legislature as a whole had little sympathy for wealthy individuals and corporations, and when the state needed revenues, this class of taxpayer was given little lenience. As the governor and the general assembly began deliberations over various possible sources of revenue, luxury taxes, state income taxes, and heavy intangibles taxes were quick to come to mind, and reactivation of the old tax was suggested as the first step in raising the funds necessary to meet the state's budget.

The law's revival made it very difficult for Georgians with any personal wealth to maintain their residences in the state, and the Woodruffs were among those who sought temporary refuge elsewhere. Robert Woodruff changed his official residence to Wilmington, Delaware, where he had moved the headquarters of The Coca-Cola Company to avoid the oppressive taxation of its holdings, and Ernest and Emily Woodruff and their youngest son, Henry, moved their official residence to Maidens, Virginia, although they returned periodically throughout their self-imposed exile to their home on Springdale Road, where they had moved from Inman Park in 1923.[53] George and Irene continued to live in Daytona Beach, with George commuting to Atlanta, Birmingham, and other cities with offices of the Continental Gin Company by train. Jane Woodruff recalled that the family had a ritual of putting George on the train every Monday morning and picking him up every Friday evening until, after several years in Florida, he began working in his office at the South Peninsula Drive house full time, traveling to Birmingham only for important meetings.[54]

Mr. and Mrs. Ernest Woodruff's golden wedding anniversary, celebrated at the Greenbriar in White Sulpher Springs, West Virginia, on April 22, 1935. Seated from left to right are George W. Woodruff, Nell Hodgson (Mrs. Robert W.) Woodruff, Ernest Woodruff, Emily Winship (Mrs. Ernest) Woodruff, Mrs. J. N. Goddard, and Ralph Hayes. First row standing, left to right are Drury Walters, Mrs. Thomas K. Glenn, Mary Frances Winship Walters, Robert W. Woodruff, Mrs. Jim Goodrum, Henry Francis Woodruff, and Thomas K. Glenn. Second row standing from left to right are Frank McGovern, Robert Strickland (in background), Cecil B. ("Abie") Cowan, John N. Goddard, Alfred Newell, and Gene Kelley. (Credit: Cummins-"The Greenbriar")

Around the time that enforcement of the intangibles tax was finally relaxed, Ernest and Emily Woodruff returned to the city on a full-time basis, although Henry retained his permanent residence at the Maidens farmhouse until his death in 1947. Robert and Nell Woodruff took up official residence in Atlanta around 1946, living two doors down from the senior Woodruffs on Springdale Road. After George and Irene bought and moved into their English tudor home at 3668 Tuxedo Road upon their return to Atlanta, Robert and Nell bought the large white house two doors down from George and Irene, and the two couples remained close and congenial neighbors for the rest of their lives.[55]

From left to right, George W. Woodruff, father Ernest Woodruff, and brother Robert W. Woodruff at a dinner celebrating the fiftieth anniversary of the Trust Company of Georgia in September of 1941. Ernest Woodruff was first elected to the board in 1893 through his connection with his brother-in-law Joel Hurt. He became president of the Trust Company in 1904 and served in that capacity until 1922, when he became chairman of the board of directors. Ernest Woodruff retired from the chairmanship in 1937 and was the guest of honor at this gathering. George Woodruff became a director in 1947 and was named an Advisory Director in 1968 when he reached mandatory retirement age. Robert Woodruff became a director in 1916 and was named Advisory Director when he reached the age of seventy-three in 1962. The family connection to the Trust Company was and is extremely strong. The Trust Company was investment banker for the Woodruff family's several related charitable trusts, as well as private trusts of individual family members. (Credit: Reeves Studios—Atlanta)

Irene and George Woodruff in front of the Christmas tree at home on Tuxedo Road in the 1950s.

Once settled in Atlanta, George Woodruff continued to commute to Birmingham when necessary, but worked most frequently at home or at his office in the Trust Company, and both George and Irene spent a good deal of time tending to the needs of their infirm fathers. Clyde King died in 1941 at the age of sixty-six, Ernest Woodruff's death at the age of eighty-one followed in 1944, and the whole family gradually returned the bulk of their energies to their usual pursuits. Irene quickly resumed her heavy schedule of civic work and family activities, while the two younger daughters attended school. Frances Woodruff, who had graduated from the Graham-Eckes School in Daytona in 1940, enrolled in Mount Vernon Junior College in Washington, D.C. She graduated in 1942, was a member of the Atlanta Debutante Club for a year, and married Robert M. Hallock in an elaborate ceremony at the First Presbyterian Church in Atlanta in 1943.[56] Jane Woodruff graduated from Washington Seminary, one of the predecessors of The Westminster Schools, in 1943. She also attended Mount Vernon Junior College, where she was active in athletics and student government, graduating in 1945. She then served as president of the Atlanta Debutante Club for the 1945-46 season and married Richard W. King in 1946 in Atlanta.[57]

George Woodruff, who had been preoccupied throughout the second world war with parental illnesses, daughters' marriages, and the Continental Gin Company, whose normally heavy production schedule had been further burdened by a commitment to manufacture bombs for the United States government, began to relax more as he continued in his usual schedule of business and civic involvement.[58] First named to the board in 1935, Woodruff continued as an active director of the Atlantic Steel Company, where he had worked as a draftsman when first married in 1918, for forty years. He also increased his advisory role at The Coca-Cola Company, where he had been appointed to the board of directors in 1936. He was later named to the Executive Committee, the Compensation Committee, and the to the Executive Committee, the Compensation Committee, and the Finance Committee, from the vantage point of which he kept a sharp eye on Company expenditures.[59] Woodruff was also made a director of Coca-Cola Interamerican Corporation, Coca-Cola, Ltd., Canada, and The Coca-Cola Export Corporation upon their formation of each.[60] He remained active as a director of The Coca-Cola Company from his election until his retirement in 1985.

George Woodruff was an extremely loyal representative of The Coca-Cola Company, and he looked out for the Company's interests wherever he went. As a director of West Point Manufacturing Company and its successor corporation, West Point-Pepperell, Inc., Woodruff would take any available opportunity to tour the company's mills, purportedly to satisfy his interest as a mechanical engineer in the operation of the mills' machinery, but primarily because of his interest as a director and major stockholder of The Coca-Cola Company in making certain that West Point-Pepperell soft drink machines stocked only Coca-Cola products.[61] Discovery that a company or an organization did not patronize The Coca-Cola Company led to Woodruff's grave disappointment, and his friend Charles L. Gowen remembered hearing of an unhappy golf outing at the East Lake Country Club, where Woodruff's foursome, having paused to refresh themselves with Coca-Cola at a drink stand after the first nine holes, were politely informed that the East Lake Country Club did not stock Coca-Cola and were offered Pepsi instead. Scandalized, Woodruff refused the proffered substitute, saying to his companions ruefully, "Just think of all my family has done for this club." Woodruff, as far as Gowen knew, chose to play golf at other clubs following the East Lake incident.[62]

It was often said of Woodruff by those who knew him that once he had made up his mind on a subject, he was absolutely unswerving. If anyone wanted to talk him out of one of his considered decisions, he would have to be thoroughly prepared on the facts, know Woodruff well, and send the right emissary to accomplish the task. Woodruff was confident of the positions he took and would back them to the extreme, and he was known for forcing organizations and businesses with which he was involved to stay true to course once they had committed to a plan. During the time he was a director of West Point Manufacturing Company, Woodruff's characteristic tenacity was demonstrated in one of the most celebrated fights for corporate control that had occurred in the South to that time. The fight began when Joseph L. Lanier, whose father and grandfather had headed the company from the time of its founding in 1880, was executive vice president of West Point Manufacturing Company, which was then in the process of merging with the New England-based Pepperell Company.[63] West Point Manufacturing Company had for many years been one of the largest employers in the Lanett Valley, and the combination of the jobs the company supplied and the general importance of the textile industry to the South made Pepperell's establishment of headquarters for the merged company in Boston a real threat to the livelihood and pride of many southerners.[64]

Preparing to mount his fight for the company, Lanier retained Robert Troutman of the law firm of King & Spalding, then Spalding, Sibley, Troutman & Kelley, to plan a legal strategy whereby control of the company could be regained from the New England interests. Lanier was supported by George Woodruff in his request, and Troutman began intensive legal research with a view toward launching a proxy fight for control of the company.

The investigation proved fruitful, producing evidence of mismanagement by the New England faction, and armed with the damaging facts, Troutman and Woodruff traveled to Boston to do battle. Woodruff, in tough and heated negotiations, confronted the officers with the evidence they had assembled and managed to secure the resignation of several top officials and three directors of the company who supported the New England faction. The negotiations produced the agreement that Lanier would become president of the company and nominate successor members to its board of directors.

On the train en route back to Atlanta, Woodruff and Troutman, both deeply religious men, knelt in prayer for guidance and support in the reconstruction of the newly dismantled board of directors. Minutes later, as they proceeded to the dining car, they happened upon William W. Wolbach, one of the successors that Lanier had previously planned to recruit, who was traveling on business. Frank P. Samford, president of Liberty Life Insurance Company of Birmingham and the second planned recruit, was in the dining car, and on their arrival in Atlanta the following morning, Troutman and Woodruff saw John A. Sibley, chairman of the board of the Trust Company of Georgia, crossing the street in front of their cab. Sibley was recruited on the spot as the third replacement director. "The prayer's what did it," Woodruff later said modestly.[65] Joe Lanier gave Woodruff a tiny gold boxing glove to commemorate the fight growing out of a merger which, until The Coca-Cola Company's acquisition of Columbia Pictures in the 1980s, was perhaps the most significant corporate acquisition in the region.[66] Woodruff wore his boxing glove memento proudly to the end of his life.

George Woodruff was an active, vocal, and knowledgeable member of the many boards on which he sat, and he served their interests with ability and dedication in the boardroom, as well as in the field. His views and experience were well-respected by his brother Robert Woodruff, and the two men communicated constantly on matters of family and business. Close employees and family members of each man recall that the brothers "adored each other" and let very few days pass without a note, a call, or a visit, if both were in the same town. Each man relied on the other's business experience and judgment, and just as Robert was an invaluable member of the board of directors of the Continental Gin Company, George was, often at Robert's urging, a director of a number of companies in which Robert had an interest.[67] The two brothers formed an impenetrable and indivisible front wherever they turned their attention, and if they ever disagreed on a matter of policy, their compromise position was

worked out between them in privacy and in advance, and no evidence of diverging views was visible to colleagues or other Board or committee members.[68]

George Woodruff was known to be an astute businessman who watched balance sheets closely, asked difficult, incisive questions, and had an unerring sense of what was and was not possible in business. Several presidents of organizations Woodruff served as a director went so far as to say that the expectation of Woodruff's habitual close reading of balance sheets, reports, and proposals was a tremendous

Brothers Robert W. and George W. Woodruff, taken in December of 1957. (Credit: Leviton—Atlanta)

Robert C. Balfour of Thomasville, Georgia, George W. Woodruff, Robert W. Woodruff, and turkey at Robert Woodruff's Ichauway Plantation in South Georgia in the 1940s.

help in preparing for a board meeting, as it encouraged a meticulously thorough and thoughtful presentation on the part of the person in charge.[69] In addition to his acuity in these areas, he was adept at working with people and could be counted upon to support management whenever a controversy arose. His opinions were highly valued, and the head of a company or school would as a matter of course seek him out ahead of time before bringing up new business or policies at a meeting of the full board in order to be certain of his approval and support.[70] Many who knew Woodruff in his capacity as a trustee or director have said that it was not at all unusual for him to stand up at a meeting and give support or commendation for an action taken or a policy adopted by management. Because of the esteem in which George Woodruff was held, such encomiums tremendously influenced other board members' views of management so assessed.[71]

Another organization that George Woodruff served faithfully over a long period of time was the Trust Company of Georgia, founded in 1891 by Woodruff's uncle, Joel Hurt, as the Commercial Traveler's Savings Bank. Ernest and Robert Woodruff also were directors of the bank, and George Woodruff's intense institutional loyalty had almost no better showcase than his relationship to the Trust Company.[72] Elected as a director in 1947, Woodruff looked after the bank's affairs with great energy, and his assumption of the role of advisory director in 1968 after his seventy-third birthday did little to dim his interest or participation.[73] Even after his ninetieth birthday, Trust Company

George W. Woodruff at the Trust Company of Georgia. This photograph was most likely taken shortly after the completion of the new Trust Company Tower next to the site of the original Trust Company Building on the northeast corner of Pryor Street (now Park Place) and Edgewood Avenue. When the tower was completed in 1970, the tenants moved there from the old building, making way for its demolition. The Trust Company of Georgia Banking Annex was then built in its place. The poster directly above Woodruff's head in the photograph shows the construction of the new banking annex in progress.

president and Sun Trust vice chairman Jimmy Williams remembered, Woodruff was still watching the bank's balance sheets closely and was vocal about expense control. Woodruff, said Williams, always advocated tough management, urging those in power to maximize earnings while keeping the balance sheet firm—not an easy compromise. His influence at the bank was quiet but effective, as bank officers realized that his preferences and advice stemmed from a sound knowledge of business and a keen interest in the Trust Company's success, an interest that was rooted, as many close to Woodruff have indicated, in his role as a customer as well as his position as a director and stockholder.

Woodruff's interest in the operation of the bank was far-ranging. Jimmy Williams remembers the years he spent in Augusta with the First National Bank and Trust Company of Augusta, noting that there were very few visitors, certainly none of Woodruff's stature with the Trust Company, from the Atlanta banking community to his bank. Woodruff, however, would visit Williams at the Augusta bank on his frequent trips to play golf at the Augusta National course, and Williams always felt that the older man was genuinely interested in all of the activities of the bank.[74]

Woodruff was as loyal a customer to the Trust Company of Georgia as he was a director, and many connected with Woodruff, Trust Company, The Coca-Cola Company, and Woodruff's many charitable concerns have contended that he was the best customer the bank ever had.[75] All of Woodruff's business centered on the Trust Company, from his personal accounts and trusts and the accounts and trusts he set up for his children and grandchildren to the accounts and trusts of his various charitable beneficiaries, whom he strongly encouraged to keep their funds with the Trust Company of Georgia.[76]

George Woodruff approached his civic and charitable involvements with the same sense of responsibility, honesty, and integrity as he did his business affiliations. Never an impulsive giver, Woodruff was known for thoroughly researching and analyzing proposals he received from various educational and charitable institutions, asking pointed questions, and studying with a keen eye the ability of the requesting body to make good use of any donated funds. Where many philanthropists might donate sums to institutions on an isolated, one-time basis, Woodruff preferred to consolidate his charities, and once he made the decision to give his support to any given institution, he remained loyal to the cause, with his interest and advisory role reaching down to students, patients, or whomever were the ultimate beneficiaries of his largesse.[77]

Although George Woodruff was known by friends and associates for being somewhat parsimonious where personal expenditures were concerned, that characteristic was a product of basic thrift and financial conservatism rather than miserliness. He was a careful accountant of his personal funds, and family servants recall with amusement his constant encouragement to save and invest their money, as well as to conserve electricity, water, and heat as they went about their work in the Woodruff household.[78] Friends and associates remember that Woodruff and the other wealthy members of his regular golf foursome would drink Coke and eat free saltine crackers in the clubhouse after a round of golf, while others of considerably less significant financial means enjoyed sandwiches, potato chips, and other items from the club's menu. At the Trust Company, Woodruff was similarly frugal, eating every day in the bank's cafeteria and purchasing his lunch with the discount card he received for being a Trust Company director.[79] The end result of his personal thrift, however, was an increased generosity to causes he considered worthy and capable of managing donated funds with a sense of thrift and responsibility commensurate with Woodruff's own.

George Woodruff became interested in the many institutions he supported in a variety of ways, often through the continuation of a pattern of giving established by family members or friends. His long relationship with Emory University is an example of an interest stemming from business as well as family tradition, as Asa G. Candler, early owner of The Coca-Cola Company, was one of the key figures in encouraging the Southern Methodist General Conference to locate its new university in Atlanta, rather than another Southern city. While the General Conference had decided to charter a university in the Southeast and was interested in locating the new college in Georgia, Conference members felt at the time that Oxford, Georgia, where tiny Emory College had been founded in 1836, was as likely a choice as Atlanta, and Atlanta's ultimate selection was in large part the result of Asa Candler's committed campaigning.

Candler's enthusiastic efforts produced from various sources offers of land for a campus, already standing buildings suitable for academic departments, a hospital around which a planned medical school could be built, various money donations, and, perhaps most influentially, an offer of a million dollar endowment for the school from Asa Candler himself.[80] While the offer, which was written in a letter now known popularly as "Asa Candler's million dollar letter," was not conditioned on where the campus was actually established, it surely added to the attraction of the other offers to make Atlanta the General Conference's choice.[81] Emory College was moved from Oxford at that time and made the undergraduate college of the new university, with the school facility in Oxford, Georgia, remaining open as a two-year liberal arts college and a unit of Emory University. Schools of Medicine, Dentistry, Nursing, Theology, Law, and Business Administration were added later to the new Atlanta campus, along with the Graduate School of Arts and Sciences.[82]

Candler's support of Emory University did not stop at the million dollar letter, and his continued financial interest in the institution began a tradition of support from those connected with The Coca-Cola Company. In 1935, Robert Woodruff was elected to the board of trustees of Emory, beginning more than fifty years of the Woodruffs' service to the university. Two years after Robert's appointment, a tragedy struck the Woodruff family, which, despite the sorrow it occasioned, was destined to benefit Emory greatly for many years to come. In 1937, Emily Woodruff was diagnosed with cancer, and at the time she became ill, there was no medical facility in the Southeast that specialized in the diagnosis and treatment of neoplastic diseases other than the Steiner Clinic at Grady Hospital, the use of which was restricted to charity patients. A short time after their mother's diagnosis, George and Robert conferred with both parents and persuaded them that neither they nor their brother Henry were in need of any inheritance and asked that the senior Woodruffs create a charitable foundation to be the beneficiary of both of their estates.[83] Emily and Ernest complied immediately, and Ernest oversaw the foundation's activities until his death in 1944, at which time George took over his father's responsibilities in administration of the foundation while serving with Robert on its board of trustees.[84]

A short time after the formation of the Emily and Ernest Woodruff Foundation, George and Robert announced plans for the establishment of the Robert Winship Memorial Clinic at Emory, a facility intended to function as an adjunct to the medical school in training as well as treatment, educating medical students in the latest techniques of cancer diagnosis and care. The clinic was to be funded by the foundation and named for Robert Winship, George and Robert Woodruff's maternal grandfather, who had died of cancer in 1899 at the age of sixty-five.[85] The advanced facilities of the Robert Winship Memorial Clinic were conceived of and completed too late to treat Emily, who died in 1939, but the clinic and the foundation that funded it were significant and lasting tributes to her memory.[86]

The wealth represented by each of the elder Woodruffs' estates was substantial, and the addition of a part of Henry Woodruff's estate at his death in 1947 increased the foundation's income by a sig-

Robert Winship Woodruff (1889-1985), Henry Francis Woodruff (1897-1947), and George Waldo Woodruff (1895-1987), sons of Ernest and Emily Winship Woodruff.

cant measure. Despite the impressive net worth of the foundation at the time it was established, however, it was the form of the wealth—stock in The Coca-Cola Company, preserved intact and rising steadily in value—that caused the foundation's corpus ultimately to reach its staggering size.[87]

The Emily and Ernest Woodruff Foundation was for over forty years a substantial source of support and growth for Emory University. George and Robert Woodruff were the foundation's two most influential trustees, and each was committed to the idea that Emory was a worthy beneficiary of the foundation's available funds. While in later years committed to supporting Emory with forty percent of its income each year, the Emily and Ernest Woodruff Foundation also made specific gifts of additional amounts to both the medical center and the university's general fund.[88] In the three decades following the

The Emory University Board of Trustees, taken January 25, 1957. Woodruff served as a trustee on this board from 1951-1965, and continued as a trustee emeritus until his death in 1987. Seated from left to right are Mr. James D. Robinson, Jr., Mr. George W. Woodruff, Dr. Noland B. Harmon, Jr., Dr. Goodrich C. White, Mr. Charles Howard Candler, Sr., Bishop Arthur J. Moore, Bishop Marvin A. Franklin, Senator Spessard L. Holland, and Mr. William N. Banks. Standing from left to right are Mr. Aubrey F. Folts, Mr. William B. Turner, Dr. F. Phinizy Calhoun, Mr. Charles M. Trammell, Mr. L. P. McCord, Mr. Granger Hansell, Mr. Henry L. Bowden, Dr. Luther A. Harrell, Mr. Harry Y. McCord, Jr., Mr. George S. Craft, Mr. Morgan S. Cantey, Mr. James C. Malone, Mr. C. Howard Candler, Jr., Mr. Harllee Branch, Jr., Dr. Embree H. Blackard, Dr. Lester A. Rumble, Mr. S. Charles Candler, Dr. Wadley R. Glenn, and Mr. F. M. Bird. Members not pictured were Mr. Angus E. Bird, Mr. James V. Carmichael, Mr. Donald S. Comer, and Bishop William T. Watkins.

creation of the foundation, gifts were made to Emory of stock in The Coca-Cola Company worth a total of over $100 million estimated as of the time they were made, although the stock's continuous and sharp rise in value makes its actual worth in Emory's portfolio incalculable.[89]

Emory's good fortune at the hands of the Emily and Ernest Woodruff Foundation, like the value of the Coca-Cola stock itself, seemed only to increase. In November of 1979, the corpus of the Emily and Ernest Woodruff Foundation, renamed the Emily and Ernest Woodruff Fund following a restructuring owing to tax considerations in 1975, was transferred to Emory University at a value of approximately $105 million.[90] As the fund's assets consisted of stock in The Coca-Cola Company, the value of the gift continued to rise in Emory's hands, and recent estimates calculate the stock's worth to be approximately $250 million.[91]

The termination of the Emily and Ernest Woodruff Fund in favor of Emory made national news as the largest single gift ever made to a university, a record only recently exceeded. George Woodruff, although not an alumnus of Emory, had served the university faithfully as a trustee from his election in 1951 and had consistently exercised his influence from his position as a trustee of the fund to support Emory. He had extreme confidence in the institution's ability to put donated funds to good use, as he respected Emory's faculty and administration, felt that the medical center was a vital asset to the region, and believed that the school's physical plant was sound. In short, Woodruff thought that of all the institutions that had received support from the time of the Fund's creation, Emory was the one that could become nationally known and respected through the use of the Woodruff money, and he therefore began to advocate strongly the transfer of the Fund to Emory.[92]

Woodruff worked to convince the other trustees of the Fund, including his brother Robert, of the soundness of his argument, as several of the trustees were content for the Fund to continue on as it was indefinitely. From the time that the Fund was restructured in 1975, it had supported Emory with forty percent of its income annually and distributed the remaining sixty percent to the trustees' choice of twenty-seven other named institutions that could receive moneys from the Fund under the Internal Revenue Service classifications for supporting organizations.[93] Other trustees were in favor of increasing Emory's dedicated portion to sixty percent, while continuing to distribute forty percent to the named institutions.[94] George Woodruff felt, however, that because he and his brother had persuaded their parents to establish the foundation initially and because George and his personal secretary had kept the organization's records and watched over its assets from the time of its inception, he and his brother had an obligation to see that the corpus of the Fund was distributed to a worthy institution while they were living.[95]

It was the 1979 Campaign for Emory that finally persuaded all of the trustees of the Emily and Ernest Woodruff Fund that the corpus of the foundation should be transferred to Emory University, as the trustees felt that a large gift at that time would encourage other large donations, thereby increasing the ultimate value of the foundation's gift to the university by a significant measure.[96] Emory had set out to raise $60 million dollars, by far the most ambitious fund-raising goal in the university's history, during the planned five-year campaign. Emory president James T. Laney, with the support of George and Robert Woodruff, had secured Emory alumnus and Trust Company of Georgia president Jimmy Williams to chair the campaign, and after the Emily and Ernest Woodruff Fund had committed to its major gift, the officers of the Campaign for Emory, one of whom was George Woodruff, immediately revised the campaign's goal upward to $160 million, and then again to $185 million. When the campaign ended on December 31, 1984, the total of gifts and pledges stood at somewhat more than $220 million, not including $17 million in bequests that the university will eventually receive.[97]

Throughout the campaign, recalled Williams, Woodruff's participation as an officer and advisor was vital to the fundraising effort. Woodruff, said Williams, knew where the money was and precisely

Portrait of George W. Woodruff with the Woodruff family crest in the background, painted by Peter Stevens in 1970. The original hangs in the Walter F. George School of Law at Mercer University, and a copy hangs over a fireplace at the Woodruff House.

how and by whom an approach to a potential donor should be made in order to secure a pledge.[98]

After the Emily and Ernest Woodruff Fund's trustees voted in favor of transferring the foundation's assets to Emory, George Woodruff went before his fellow members of Emory's board of trustees to announce the foundation's plan. Obviously pleased, Woodruff spoke with a great sense of determination and pride. "My brother and I have decided to give the foundation's assets to Emory," Woodruff began before reading the prepared statement from the foundation's letterhead concerning the transfer of the Fund to the university.[99] After forty-two years of support to health, education, and the arts, George and Robert Woodruff felt that the fund had fulfilled its obligation to the general community and that Emory would be a good steward for the benefit of the public through the application of the corpus of the Fund to improvements to its medical and educational programs.[100] In addition to its support of schools, medical facilities, and community centers, the foundation had also made a number of high-profile gifts over the years, including more than $19 million to help build and maintain the Atlanta Memorial Arts Center and $13 million to the City of Atlanta to purchase the block of low-rise buildings that were cleared to create Central City Park and the adjoining small amphitheater near Five Points, both of which were renamed Robert W. Woodruff Park in 1985.[101] The conveyance to Emory of the Fund's corpus, which was held in the form of stock in Coca-Cola International Corporation, was completed in 1980.[102]

In 1980, Emory University, in appreciation of George Woodruff's long service as a trustee of the university, a spokesman in Emory's behalf on the board of trustees of the Emily and Ernest Woodruff Foundation, and a tireless fundraiser in the Campaign for Emory, awarded Woodruff an honorary Doctor of Laws degree at the May commencement ceremony. As Emory president James Laney tells the story, Woodruff had been extremely ill for some time and was recovering from major surgery at Emory University Hospital when commencement was scheduled. University regulations required the presence of any degree candidates at commencement, so Woodruff and Laney agreed prior to the ceremony that Woodruff, whose G-wing hospital room overlooked the university quadrangle where the commencement ceremony was to be held, would at some time during the service come to the window of his room and look out over the crowd. Below, at the ceremony, Dr. Laney announced to the assemblage when Woodruff's degree was conferred, "Mr. Woodruff cannot be with us on the stage today, but he is present with us in the quadrangle."[103]

In May of 1981, Emory broke ground for the George W. Woodruff Physical Education Center, a $10 million athletic complex designed by Atlanta architect John Portman and built to replace Emory's old gymnasium, which had opened in 1948 and been renovated and expanded only minimally in the ensuing years. The center was the first construction project to be funded by the proceeds of the

George Woodruff and Emory president James T. Laney shooting baskets in the newly opened George W. Woodruff Physical Education Center.

(Credit: Ann Youngling)

Dr. William C. McGarity, George W. Woodruff, and Dr. Stephen W. Schwarzman. Woodruff endowed chairs at Emory University in honor of the two Emory doctors.

Campaign for Emory and was named to honor George Woodruff for his service to the school before and during the campaign.[104]

In October of 1983, George Woodruff announced to Emory his decision to establish the Stephen W. Schwarzman Chair of Internal Medicine and the William C. McGarity Chair of Surgery to honor the two physicians, Dr. William McGarity and Dr. Steve Schwarzmann, who had cared for him through serious illnesses in 1974, 1980, and 1983. Woodruff endowed the chairs with one million dollars each, and was not hesitant to remark that the chairs were a small measure of the gratitude he felt for the men he said saved his life on three separate occasions. Woodruff was also the primary source of support for Emory's Enterostomal Therapy Educational Program, which trained registered nurses to care for and rehabilitate ostomal patients, from the time of the program's foundation in 1976.[105] On Woodruff's ninety-first birthday, Emory University held a ground breaking ceremony for the George and Irene Woodruff Residential Center, and Woodruff, after thanking Emory for "all the fuss" of the groundbreaking celebration and birthday party, called Dr. Laney to the podium to present him with a million dollar check to help maintain the facility. "I have already given you a lot of money to pay for this building," Woodruff said, "but here is a check to add to it."

Another institution that benefited greatly from the generosity of the Woodruff family over the years is the Henrietta Egleston Hospital for Children, an affiliate of the Emory University School of Medicine, located on Emory's campus. Now recognized as one of the finest tertiary care facilities for children in the country, Egleston was founded in 1928 with a $100,000 posthumous grant by Thomas Egleston as a memorial to his mother. The first Egleston facility was located on Forrest Avenue in Atlanta, and there, the fifty-bed hospital battled common childhood maladies of pellegra, rickets, and scurvy. By 1959, Egleston had outgrown its Forrest Avenue home and relocated to more spacious quarters on the Emory campus.[106]

Egleston Hospital was Irene Woodruff's special interest over a period of more than thirty years as she volunteered every Sunday afternoon to work among the children and their parents at the hospital. Irene had always loved children, and with little Irene, Frances, and Jane grown, her work at Egleston was a welcome opportunity to maintain contact with young people. Irene chose to volunteer her time on Sunday afternoons, feeling that many volunteers with young children of their own would want to be at home with them during those hours.[107] In a 1981 tribute to Irene's long service to Egleston, Louise Allen, wife of former Atlanta mayor Ivan Allen, Jr., and then member of Egleston's advisory board, shared the recollection of an Egleston staff member:

Irene King Woodruff in a volunteer nurse's uniform at Egleston Hospital for Children, reading to a patient and her mother. While both Mr. and Mrs. Woodruff had an enduring interest in and loyalty to Egleston Hospital, Mrs. Woodruff enjoyed giving her time as much as she did her funds. She was a common sight at the hospital, especially on Sunday afternoons, when other volunteers were unavailable, said family friend and Egleston board chairman Alfred D. Boylston, Jr.

> One of Egleston's long-time employees characterized Mrs. Woodruff's love and concern more beautifully than I can express it.
>
> She tells the story of a strapping young man dressed in mechanics's clothes, wringing his hands helplessly, with a frightened and bewildered young wife holding the baby as Mrs. Woodruff carries their luggage down an Egleston hallway to the child's room, assuring the parents every step of the way that everything will be okay. This is a typical picture of Mrs. Woodruff on a Sunday afternoon at Egleston year after year.[108]

On their fiftieth wedding anniversary in April of 1968, George Woodruff established the Irene King Woodruff Fund at Egleston to honor Irene, and Alfred D. Boylston, Jr., longtime Woodruff friend and Honorary Chairman of Egleston's board of trustees, in 1986 estimated George and Irene's total gifts to the hospital at over $13 million. In 1981, a $25 million addition to the hospital was opened and named the George and Irene Woodruff Pavilion to honor the Woodruffs' many years of support to Egleston.[109]

Through his entire life, George Woodruff remained loyal to Georgia Tech, his *alma mater,* and prior to the termination of the

Agnes Scott College president Ruth A. Schmidt hands George Woodruff a hard hat inscribed with his name at a groundbreaking ceremony on the Agnes Scott College campus. (Credit: Ann States)

Emily and Ernest Woodruff Fund, he represented Tech's interests strongly in his role as the Fund's vice-chairman. He was for forty-four years a trustee of the Georgia Tech Foundation, a body created in 1932 for the purpose of keeping gifts made to the school, which is a unit of the University System of Georgia, separate from funds the state makes available to Tech. In 1943, the foundation was reconstituted and charged with the additional responsibilities of fundraising and allocating the raised funds to the university's building and improvement projects.[110] George Woodruff was a charter trustee of the newly reorganized foundation and took great pride as it raised money to expand and improve the university's facilities and programs, starting in 1932 with assets of $200,000 and growing to over $30 million at the time of Woodruff's death.[111] Through the Emily and Ernest Woodruff Foundation and the Georgia Tech Foundation, Woodruff worked to establish an endowment for scholarship funds for National Merit scholars, a program for students who play non-revenue producing sports, and an endowed chair in micro-electronics. He also gave personally and extensively through the Georgia Tech alumni giving program, and Irene Woodruff left Tech approximately $1 million at her death in 1982.[112] In 1978, Woodruff transferred his house at 3668 Tuxedo Road to Tech, retaining a life estate.[113]

On his seventy-second birthday, Woodruff became an emeritus trustee of the foundation, but the change in official status did not affect his commitment to the university. In gratitude for Woodruff's continued support, Georgia Tech presented Woodruff with the Alumni Distinguished Service Award in 1963, and in 1983, Woodruff received the Georgia Tech Alumni Association Thousand Club Award for Exceptional Service. A new dormitory was named for George and Irene Woodruff in 1984, and in 1985, the George W. Woodruff School of Mechanical Engineering was dedicated to honor the contributions of the man who had been an eager student in that program more than seventy years earlier.

Despite his constant attention to Tech's financial affairs over the years, Woodruff's loyalty to Georgia Tech went beyond a cool and businesslike interest in the university's expansion and improvement. He held season tickets for Tech Yellow Jacket football games for seventy-two years and attended games up until the fall before his death.

As with Rabun Gap-Nachoochee School, Emory University and Georgia Tech, George Woodruff became involved in supporting Agnes Scott College through a long heritage of family commitment to the school. Clara Belle Rushton King, Irene Woodruff's mother, had attended Agnes Scott College from 1892 through 1894, when she married Clyde King, and Mary Frances Winship, George Woodruff's maternal aunt and his daughter Frances's namesake, was her close friend and classmate there.[114] "Mary Frank," as Frances was known by her contemporaries, was one of Clara Belle's six bridesmaids in her 1894 wedding, and the two women, along with three other alumnae of Agnes Scott and two more of their friends, called themselves the Seven Mystic Maids and remained close throughout their lives. Over the years they would gather to celebrate their birthdays and other significant occasions, recording photographically almost thirty years of their meetings.[115] Frances Winship, later Mrs. George C. Walters, actively supported Agnes Scott throughout her life and left four million dollars to the college at her death in 1954.[116] Clara Belle King was also an active alumnae, giving George and Irene a strong incentive on each side of the family to take an interest in Agnes Scott.

Founded in 1889 in Decatur under the auspices of the Decatur Presbyterian Church, Agnes Scott College was the product of many community leaders' belief in a need for the establishment of a Christian school for women. Colonel George Washington Scott, one such community leader, played a key part in the founding of the Decatur Female Seminary, which was opened to a student body of sixty-three and a faculty of four on September 24, 1889, a scant month after the founders' organizational meeting. Not long after the school opened, the name was changed from Decatur Female Seminary to Agnes Scott College in honor of Colonel Scott's mother, Agnes Irvine Scott.[117]

George Woodruff began his official relationship with Agnes Scott in 1939, when he was asked to serve on the board of trustees of the college. He was a trustee from 1939 through 1942, at which time he stepped down from the board for five years. In 1947, he reassumed his position as trustee and served in that capacity until 1955, when he was named vice chairman of the board of trustees.[118] Early in 1956, after Woodruff had been vice chairman of the board for only several months, he was asked to stand in for then chairman George Winship, his mother's first cousin, who was terminally ill, and after acting as chairman for several months, Woodruff guided the board and the college in taking one of the strongest stands on academic freedom in Agnes Scott's history.[119] Then college president Wallace M. Alston had, in keeping with the usual practice of Agnes Scott, invited the 1956 baccalaureate speaker well in advance of the baccalaureate ceremony, but a controversy arose over Alston's selected speaker, eminent theologian and Professor of Philosophica Theology in Vanderbilt University's Divinity School, Nels F. S. Ferre. Two longtime trustees of the college asked President Alston to cancel the eminent professor's invitation on the grounds that his beliefs, doctrines, and writings were not theologically "sound." Woodruff, recognizing the two trustees' persistence and the seriousness of their complaints, appointed a special faculty committee to "study criticisms of the writings of Dr. Ferre and to consider the advisability of his appearing for his engagement in June."[120]

The results of the study were presented to the full board at its annual meeting on May 11, 1956, where the committee recommended that Professor Ferre's invitation to speak remain open. The committee concluded that Agnes Scott College's purpose and function as a liberal arts institution with an avowed Christian commitment made necessary a particularly difficult balancing of apparently opposing ideals. Under acting chairman Woodruff's leadership, the board of trustees captured the essence of that critical offset of values in what was to be the college's first statement on academic freedom, passed as a resolution at the May 1956 annual meeting:

> We are proud of a tradition that assumes and safeguards the freedom of the faculty members to think, to speak, to write, and to act. It is expected that faculty members will exercise this freedom with due regard for the purposes and ideals of the college, with common sense, and with a maturity that discriminates between the irresponsibility of license and the responsibility of true liberty.[121]

George Woodruff continued his service as vice chairman of the board of trustees after a new chairman was appointed until May of 1961, when he returned to his position as trustee. In November of 1974, he was named trustee emeritus, a position that he held until his death. Even after he became a trustee emeritus, however, Wood-

George W. Woodruff and Westminster president Donn M. Gaebelein at the dedication of the George W. Woodruff Library at Westminster, September 17, 1985.

ruff remained an active member of Agnes Scott's Investment Committee, a body which he had also at one time chaired.

In addition to the thoughtful and foresightful guidance he offered the college through his years as a trustee, Woodruff also was generous in his financial support. He played a key role in increasing the college's endowment and gave freely to help purchase major laboratory equipment, renovate the library, and air condition many campus buildings.[122] At her death in 1982, Irene Woodruff left $1 million to endow a financial aid fund for Agnes Scott's Return to College Program, which provides for women who have not earned a college degree to begin college work at an individualized pace, taking anywhere from one course to a full load. In October of 1985, in gratitude for George Woodruff's many years of guidance and financial support and Irene Woodruff's generous bequest, the board of trustees passed a resolution to rename the Main Quadrangle of the College as the George Waldo and Irene King Woodruff Quadrangle to honor Agnes Scott College's valued friends and benefactors.[123]

George Woodruff developed an interest in The Westminster Schools through several different connections, including the early participation in the school's fundraising efforts by friends and business associates, but his strong and longterm allegiance to the school stemmed primarily from the attendance of several of his grandchildren and great-grandchildren, to whom he was unabashedly devoted. Although the grandchildren experienced mixed academic success, Woodruff continued to support the school with great generosity and enthusiasm, and any difficulties the children had seemed even to intensify Woodruff's respect for Westminster as an institution of uncompromising standards.[124]

Dr. William L. Pressly, who was president of Westminster during the attendance of several of the Woodruff grandchildren, marveled at Woodruff's tremendous objectivity where the school was concerned. If one of the children faced academic trouble, Dr. Pressly later remembered, he would approach Woodruff with great trepidation to inform him of the situation. Woodruff always put Pressly at ease immediately, however, telling him to treat the children fairly, as he would treat any other students. Woodruff's beneficence toward Westminster was in no way conditioned upon his grandchildren's success at the school, yet when they did do well, no one was more proud of them than Woodruff himself. At the graduation of one of his great-grandchildren, which Woodruff, not well at the time, had attended with great difficulty, Dr. Pressly greeted him and remarked on his attendance with surprise and pleasure. "If I hadn't had a car," Woodruff replied gruffly "I would have crawled over."[125]

While Westminster as it exists today dates back only to 1953, the institution traces its roots to much earlier points of origin. The North Avenue Presbyterian School, later renamed The Napsonian School, was founded in 1909, and in 1951, the Napsonian trustees incorporated their school as a nonprofit, nonsectarian institution with a multi-denominational board of trustees. At that time, the institution was renamed The Westminster Schools, and Dr. Pressly, the founding president and driving force behind the newly reconstituted school, began a long process of pushing Westminster toward national recognition for its superior academic programs. In 1953, Westminster grew by another large measure as it merged with Washington Seminary, a school founded in 1878 by two grandnieces of George Washington.[126] Both Irene Woodruff and her mother, Clara Belle King, had attended Washington Seminary through high school, and Jane Woodruff continued the tradition, graduating from the school in 1943. When the Woodruff grandchildren enrolled at Westminster in the late 1950s, they became the fourth generation of the family to be included in the Washington Seminary/Westminster tradition.[127]

From the time he first became interested in Westminster, Woodruff supported the school with commitment, and it is widely said among those familiar with the school's fundraising efforts that Woodruff has been Westminister's largest single benefactor. In 1981, The Westminster Schools dedicated a new elementary school building, naming it the Irene and George Woodruff Elementary School in honor of the Woodruffs' many contributions to Westminster, and in September of 1985, Westminster opened the George W. Woodruff Library, a facility which included a library, four science labs, a computer lab, classrooms, and music rooms. Woodruff spoke at the dedication ceremony for the library of his great pride in Westminster for its excellent faculty, beautiful facilities, and astute leaders. He called the school's decision to name the new facility for him "an honor so high I can hardly reach it," and called Donn Gaebelein, president of the school, to the podium to present him with a check for $1 million to help pay the cost of maintaining the new building.

When the George W. Woodruff Library was opened in September of 1985, a bust of Woodruff, commissioned by Mercer University and executed by Glynn Acree of Atlanta in 1984, was placed in the entrance of the library. The bust was a good representation of Woodruff, who through his many years of beneficent and unpretentious interest in the school had in the students' eyes become the image of "Westminster's Grandfather." As the seasons changed, they dressed the bust in hats and scarves to suit the weather and sent photographs of the kindly and sportily-clad figure to the real Mr. George, to his great amusement.[128]

Where George Woodruff was a kindly grandfather to the elementary and junior high school students at Westminster, he was a businessman, wise investor, and astute planner to the law students at Mercer University's Walter F. George School of Law. Named life trustee of the Walter F. George School of Law Foundation in 1965, Woodruff was immediately elected treasurer of the organization and served in that capacity until his retirement from the board in 1986. He also became a member of the Finance Committee and from that vantage point supervised the investment of the foundation's assets as they grew quickly and steadily in value over the twenty-one year period of his service. Woodruff became involved in the George Foundation through the urging of John A. Sibley, for many years chairman of the board of the Trust Company of Georgia and Woodruff's longtime friend and business associate. Sibley had been a moving force behind the formation of the George Foundation, and he very much wanted his friend's guidance in the management of the foundation's assets.

On April 17, 1947, after Mercer law graduate Senator Walter F. George had been in office for twenty-five years, Mercer University's Law School was renamed the Walter F. George School of Law in ceremonies held in the chapel on the Mercer University campus. Pleased by the name change, a number of the senator's friends and admirers gathered together in the months following the ceremonies to further honor Senator George's long service to the state by establishing an endowment fund to produce income to enrich the performance of the newly renamed law school. Shortly after the fund was established, the Walter F. George School of Law Foundation was created to raise additional funds for the endowment and invest those funds for the purpose of assisting the law school in its operation and improvement.[129]

Bust of George W. Woodruff in the George W. Woodruff Library of The Westminster Schools, as dressed by the Middle School students.

By the early 1970s, Mercer law students and programs had far outgrown their facilities on campus, and various alumni of the Walter F. George School of Law joined with the trustees of the George Foundation in a search for a new building to house the law school. A brief investigation was made into the old Sears building in downtown Macon as a possible site for relocation, as Sears had plans to move its retail operations to a mall on the outskirts of town, but the ideal structure soon presented itself in the form of the Insurance Company of North America Building, which had been built in 1954 on Georgia Avenue in the center of Macon's historical district.[130] The INA Building was a replica of Independence Hall in Philadelphia and had been built two and one half times to scale, a size which was as undesirable to INA as it was attractive to Mercer. INA had designed the 90,000 square foot building with the expectation of employing a large clerical force, but the advent of computers severely contracted their personnel requirements, and the space in the new building was grossly underutilized. Fearful of creating panic among the employees whom it hoped to relocate to another building, INA management began to approach selected buyers discreetly, offering the building for $3,800,000.[131]

John A. Sibley and George W. Woodruff in the drawing room of the Woodruff House at the dedication of the Woodruff House and the Sibley Institute of Public Affairs of Mercer University, May 6, 1983.

With its marble interior, sweeping lawn, and fifteen columns representing the fifteen states in existence when INA was chartered in Philadelphia in 1792, the INA Building was a beautiful structure, and Mercer officials, the trustees of the George Foundation, and several alumni of the law school began to investigate the possibilities of Mercer's acquisition of the facility with great interest.[132] The $3,800,000 asking price, however, represented a powerful deterrent to then Mercer president Dr. Rufus C. Harris, who felt that the building was beyond Mercer's financial means. Walter F. George School of Law alumnus Robert L. Steed, however, believed that an arrangement could be struck with INA, but before exploring the possibilities, he took George Woodruff and John Sibley to inspect and approve the building.[133]

Both men were extremely impressed with the facility, thought it would be an ideal home for the Walter F. George School of Law, and enthusiastically endorsed further investigations into securing the building for Mercer. Sibley, at a meeting of the George Foundation, suggested to Dr. Harris that a committee be appointed to study the possibilities of acquiring the building. At Sibley's suggestion, George Foundation member William P. Simmons was asked to chair the committee and Steed, who had previously headed an *ad hoc* committee to investigate the desirability and feasibility of acquiring the facility, was also asked to serve. The Emily and Ernest Woodruff Fund, at the request of George Woodruff, had already committed to a grant of $500,000 for a new law building, and Steed set out at Woodruff's and Sibley's request to see what could be done to purchase the INA building at a price closer to the amount represented by the Woodruff grant than to INA's asking price.

Steed, a partner in the Atlanta firm of King & Spalding, consulted with various tax lawyers at the firm and came up with a part gift-part sale arrangement whereby INA would donate a large portion of appraised value of the building to Mercer University and receive a tax deduction for a percentage of that amount. With the right appraisal on the INA building and grounds, the benefit of the deduction, when added to the actual purchase price paid to INA by Mercer, would equal INA's original asking price of $3,800,000, while Mercer would receive title to the facility for $1,000,000, a seemingly miniscule price for a building with a replacement value estimated to exceed $7,000,000. The success of the committee's plan depended upon an appraisal for $5,400,000, and John Zellars, president of Atlanta Federal Bank, now Georgia Federal Bank, was able to obtain an appraisal of $5,700,000 for the building.[134]

Pleased with the outcome of the exploratory committee's efforts, Woodruff and Sibley asked Dr. Harris at a meeting of the George Foundation if Mercer would commit to raise the money necessary to renovate the facility into a law school in the event that funds should be made available to Mercer to make up the $1,000,000 adjusted purchase price for the INA building. Harris readily agreed that Mercer would undertake the financial commitment of the restoration, and Woodruff, smiling, then announced that the Emily and Ernest Woodruff Fund would make another $500,000 available for the purchase of the building in addition to the $500,000 already promised to Mercer. Woodruff later made a personal gift of $87,000 toward the restoration fund.[135] The part gift-part sale arrangement was approved by Mercer's trustees in September of 1976, and the Walter F. George School of Law moved into its new home in early January of 1978.[136]

In gratitude for Woodruff's financial and advisory support to Mercer through his years of service on the George Foundation and his special role in the acquisition of the INA Building, Woodruff was awarded an honorary Doctor of Laws degree at the ceremony for the dedication of the new law school building in early May of 1979. Steed, who was able to arrange the part gift-part sale with INA, was also awarded a degree, as were INA chairman and chief executive officer Ralph E. Saul and then Chief Justice of the U. S. Supreme Court Warren E. Burger, who was the featured speaker at the dedication ceremony. At the time the degree was conferred, Woodruff had never received a diploma from any institution of higher learning, and he called Steed the day after the ceremony to ask him if he had examined his diploma to see whether it specifically noted anywhere that the degree was honorary. Steed replied that he had not, and Woodruff said,

Robert L. Steed, Ralph S. Saul, George W. Woodruff, former U.S. Attorney General Griffin B. Bell, and former Chief Justice of the U.S. Supreme Court Warren E. Burger at the dedication of the Walter F. George School of Law, May 4, 1979. Steed, Saul, and Burger were awarded honorary Doctor of Laws degrees at the ceremony, where Burger was the featured speaker.

"Well, I have. And it doesn't say honorary anywhere. I wonder if I could practice law."[137] Sentimental and immensely gratified by the degree, Woodruff asked Steed if he could keep the hood he wore with his academic gown at the ceremony, and Steed, on behalf of Mercer, assured him that he could.

Shortly after the Walter F. George School of Law moved to its new quarters, Mercer officials became interested in enlarging the law school's new campus through the purchase of Overlook Mansion, an 1836 Greek Revival home built at the top of Coleman Hill on the land adjoining the new law school's property. The mansion had for years been the home of Stratford Academy, a private Macon secondary and high school, but Stratford had moved to larger quarters in 1974, leaving Overlook, its land, and its many outbuildings in a state of vacancy and massive disrepair.[138] Excited at the prospect of more than doubling the new law school campus, Mercer officials approached George Woodruff to see whether the Emily and Ernest Woodruff Fund would be willing to assist the school in the purchase of Overlook Mansion for Stratford Academy's asking price of $450,000. Mercer Development officer Harold S. Logan and Steed proposed to Woodruff that the mansion be acquired, restored, and used to house the John Adams Sibley Institute for Public Affairs, using the refurbished facility for receptions, seminars, workshops, and meetings. The mansion was to be renamed the "Woodruff House" and was also to be the home of the Walter F. George School of Law Foundation Trustee Room.[139] Woodruff was very much in favor of the idea of honoring his lifelong friend and associate and easily convinced his and

John A. Sibley and George W. Woodruff, lifelong friends and members together of several different boards of directors and trustees, including the Emily and Ernest Woodruff Foundation, the Walter F. George Foundation, The Coca-Cola Company, and the Trust Company of Georgia. They are pictured together here at the dedication of the Sibley Horticulture Building at Callaway Gardens. Sibley *became president and chairman of the board of the Trust Company of Georgia in 1946 after the sudden deaths of Robert Strickland and Thomas K. Glenn, who had held those two positions respectively from 1937 through 1946. Glenn had also been chairman of the board of Atlantic Steel at the time George Woodruff worked with the company as a draftsman from 1919-21. Mr. Woodruff also became a member of the board of directors of Atlantic Steel in 1934.*

The Woodruff House at Mercer University, dedicated in May of 1983 to house the John A. Sibley Institute for Public Affairs. The purchase and interior restoration of the 1836 Greek Revival mansion were made possible through gifts from George Woodruff and the Emily and Ernest Woodruff Foundation. Both George Woodruff and John A. Sibley were honored in the dedication of the Woodruff House and the Sibley Institute for Public Affairs for their service as directors of the Walter F. George Foundation, organized in 1947 to help support Mercer Law School.

Sibley's fellow trustees of the Emily and Ernest Woodruff Fund to make money available to Mercer for the acquisition of the mansion.

A short time after the purchase contract was signed, Steed made arrangements with the City of Macon through its mayor, Buckner Melton, whereby Mercer would deed the house and grounds to the city in exchange for the city's promise to use certain funds it had available for the Woodruff House's restoration and to permit joint use of the mansion for city and Mercer functions. Certain restrictions were placed in the deed of gift to the City of Macon, including a reversionary clause which provided that the property would be returned to Mercer University should the city fail to restore the mansion completely within a period of two years, or, if following the restoration, the city did not maintain the mansion and use it for the purposes Mercer had proposed.[140]

The more than $250,000 that the City of Macon had to spend on the renovations barely restored the Woodruff House's exterior, so

Mercer, with the blessing of city officials, caused the reverter in the deed to the city to be triggered, and the Woodruff House returned to Mercer's hands. George Woodruff then worked through the Emily and Ernest Woodruff Fund to provide Mercer with $250,000 toward the Woodruff House's restoration, the funds for which were made available in connection with the transfer of the corpus of the foundation to Emory.[141]

The restoration of the Woodruff House was completed in the spring of 1983, and dedication ceremonies were held on May 7, 1983. The mansion's interior had been elegantly decorated and furnished by Doris Moughon Schuler of Birmingham, Alabama, whose family was related to a former owner of the home. Mrs. Schuler, who was in her eighties at the time she decorated the Woodruff House, met George Woodruff for the first time at the dedication ceremonies. Crossing the room to where she stood, Woodruff, himself eighty-eight at the time, took her hand in both of his hands and smiled. "This is the most beautiful house I've ever seen," he said.[142] Later, at the dedication ceremony, Mercer officials announced the establishment of the George W. Woodruff Medal of Excellence to be awarded each year to the student who has maintained the highest academic average in the law school. The medal was designed and executed by Mercer University art professor Marshall Daugherty and was awarded for the first time at the 1984 graduation exercises for the law school.[143]

During Mercer's 1983 Sesquicentennial Campaign, George Woodruff made a commitment to the Walter F. George School of Law that exceeded the level of all gifts and sponsorships to that point. Former U. S. Attorney General Griffin B. Bell, Steed's law partner and a Mercer law graduate, joined with Steed in a proposal on behalf of the Walter F. George Foundation that Woodruff consider making provisions for a bequest to the law school's endowment fund in the range of $3,000,000 to $5,000,000. Such a gift, Bell and Steed wrote in a letter to Woodruff, "would . . . in relative terms . . . have as great a beneficial impact on the Law School now and in the years to come as did the gift of the corpus of the Emily and Ernest Woodruff Fund to Emory University some years back."[144] The solicitation by Bell and Steed received a favorable review by Woodruff, and ultimately bore fruit in the form of the largest bequest ever received by Mercer University. In August of 1984, in appreciation of his important role in the advancement of Mercer's law school, Mercer unveiled a bust of George Woodruff created for display in the Woodruff House by sculptor Glynn Acree on commission by Mercer. Full-scale reproductions of the bust are displayed at Emory, Georgia Tech, Westminster, and the Trust Company of Georgia.

While Woodruff invested a great deal of his time in the many charitable and corporate boards he served throughout his life, he also found time to spend with his family, which, through the forties and early fifties, expanded significantly with the arrival of his seven grandchildren. Irene and Alfred Michael had a daughter, Irene

Woodruff Michael, whom Woodruff immediately and permanently christened Dutsie, while Frances and Bob Hallock had four children—Robert M. Hallock, Jr., George Woodruff Hallock, Martha Virginia Hallock, nicknamed Missie by Woodruff, and Dorothy Nell Hallock. Jane and Dick King had two sons, Richard Woodruff King, called Buck by the family, and John Woodruff King.

Daw-Daw and Sweetie, as the grandchildren addressed George and Irene, loved their grandchildren and showered them with time and attention. Missie later remembered Christmases at the house on Tuxedo Road with so many gifts that it would take each family three or four trips to transport all of their presents home. While Irene planned the occasions and did all of the shopping herself, Woodruff was an eager participant in the spirit of the holiday in his own particular way. After all of the toys had been opened and appreciated, Woodruff would hand the children, grandchildren, and sons-in-law envelopes containing checks or substantial gifts of stock in The Coca-Cola Company.[145] Christmas was not the year's only occasion for gift-giving, and the grandchildren looked forward eagerly to their birthdays as well. The sixteenth birthday especially was an important rite of passage in the family, as Woodruff, who loved to tinker with engines and often worked on his own cars himself, would insist that each grandchild learn to change a tire and clean an engine. When the skills were learned, Woodruff would present the grateful grandchild with a new car and a gas card to finance its fuel.[146]

Despite the family's closeness, however, there were some times of internal strife, which, because of the family's prominence, were often played out before the public in the newspapers. During the 1960s, Frances divorced Bob Hallock and Jane divorced Dick King, and each of the women resumed the use of the Woodruff name, as did the Hallock and King children. Some years after her divorce from Bob Hallock, further family difficulties caused Woodruff's estrangement from Frances, her two sons, and her youngest daughter, although Woodruff was very close to the rest of his children and grandchildren for the remainder of his life.

On Christmas Day in 1982, Irene King Woodruff, George Woodruff's wife of sixty-four years, died at Emory University Hospital at the age of eighty-four. In their more than half century of marriage, Irene had been George's closest friend and companion in addition to his beloved spouse, and their adoring relationship was legendary among friends and acquaintances. George, friends and family members recalled, fought throughout their marriage against spending even a single night away from her, and she was devoted to the project of making his life happy and comfortable. While the good-natured teasing that began in their courtship continued throughout their long relationship, their union was reinforced with an underlying respect and loyalty that transcended any assaults from family difficulties. When Irene died, George was devastated, and although he continued his participation in the various academic, charitable, and corporate boards on which he had remained active, he never completely regained his cheerful interest in his friends, family, and surroundings.[147] For all of their married life, it had been Irene who had coaxed Woodruff, a confirmed homebody, to entertain friends, attend parties, and remain active socially. Without Irene's insistent encouragement, Woodruff, missing her greatly, was content to retreat into a quiet and isolated life at home.[148]

Several years prior to Irene's death, Woodruff, who had sold the Continental Gin Company to Allied Products of Chicago in 1959 and had retired from an active role on most of his corporate boards some time thereafter, finally began to allow the schools and other interests he had supported personally and through the Emily and Ernest Woodruff Foundation to recognize his many contributions. While Robert and George Woodruff had both traditionally insisted on anonymity in their various philanthropies, the name "Mr. Anonymous," often applied to Robert by the press, was actually far more descriptive of George. Always fearful that his wife, children, or grandchildren would become targets of cruel or desperate individuals should his family wealth be disclosed, George habitually hid from public view whenever he, either in his individual capacity or through the Emily and Ernest Woodruff Foundation, made a major gift.[149]

In addition to his concern for the safety of his family, Woodruff's requirement of privacy in his giving stemmed from a strong sense of dignified modesty. His philanthropies arose from a sincere interest in the success of the institutions he served and a genuine desire to be helpful, and his satisfaction in giving was derived from the realization of the enormous inherent worth of his support, rather than public recognition.[150] Late in his life, however, Woodruff began to accept the thanks of the various institutions that had benefited from his generosity and was proud of the many facilities that were named for him and the awards that he received.

George Woodruff was a man of plain speech, clear thought, and unquestionable integrity and honor, and he was sought after as a leader both for his experience and his unimpeachable character.[151] He was an astute judge of people and had a keen sense of perspective that was invaluable to the course of the many institutions he helped to guide through times of conflict.[152] In his leadership of the schools and foundations he supported, he would push steadily for growth, constantly urging the idea that the purpose of fundraising and sound financial management was to enhance and enrich, rather than merely to support existing programs.[153]

Despite his strength, however, Woodruff had an extremely kind side. He was a gentle man of great good humor, and those who knew him remember his warm, strong handshake and twinkling eyes.[154] He lived in relative simplicity, and several people recalled with amusement that in his later years, when he was no longer able to drive himself and was forced to employ a chauffer, Woodruff insisted on riding in the front seat of the car, next to the chauffer, avoiding the formality of the back seat.[155] His common touch and sincere interest in others enabled him to span vast distances of years and social position to make contact with people who were universally warmed by his genuine graciousness.

George Woodruff had a unique combination of compassion and capacity that singularly suited him to his role as one of the South's greatest philanthropists. As one who recognized the needs of worthy institutions and possessed the financial means to meet those needs, Woodruff greatly advanced the resources and capabilities of many medical and educational institutions throughout the Southeast. Those institutions, in their continuing promotion of the welfare of the region, are Woodruff's most fitting memorial.

ENDNOTES

¹John A. Streun, "Brief History of Cotton Gin Developments," unpublished manuscript from the files of Vela Rocker, George W. Woodruff's secretary.

²Encyclopedia Britannica (1960), Vol. 23, p. 584.

³Streun, "Brief History."

⁴Ibid.

⁵Personal interview with George W. Woodruff, 20 May 1986.

⁶*The Atlanta Journal,* 23 February 1930.

⁷Personal interview with George W. Woodruff, 7 October 1986.

⁸*The Atlanta Journal,* 23 February 1930.

⁹Personal interview with George W. Woodruff, 7 October 1986.

¹⁰*The Atlanta Journal,* 23 February 1930.

Personal interview with George W. Woodruff, 7 October 1986.

Personal interview with Joseph W. Jones, 3 October 1986.

¹¹Personal interview with George W. Woodruff, 7 October 1986. Information was also gathered from various promotional leaflets, advertisements, pictures, and other literature produced by the Continental Gin Company between 1926 and 1959, in the possession of Vela Rocker, George W. Woodruff's personal secretary from 1959 until his death in February of 1987.

¹²Personal interview with George W. Woodruff, 7 October 1986.

¹³Ibid.

¹⁴Personal interview with George W. Woodruff, 10 October 1986.

¹⁵Personal interview with George W. Woodruff, 7 October 1986.

¹⁶Personal interview with George W. Woodruff, 20 May 1986.

Woodruff home movies compiled for George W. Woodruff's ninetieth birthday party at Emory University, 27 August 1985, are in the possession of Jane Woodruff.

¹⁷Personal interview with George W. Woodruff, 20 May 1986.

¹⁸Ibid.

[19] Personal interview with Jane Woodruff, 10 October 1986.

[20] Ibid.

[21] Ibid.

[22] Ibid.

[23] Personal interview with Robert M. Hallock and Martha W. Raudabaugh, 31 July 1986.

[24] Personal interview with Joe Jones, 3 October 1986.

[25] Personal interview with George W. Woodruff, 20 May 1986.

[26] Personal interview with George W. Woodruff, 31 December 1986.

Personal interview with Robert M. Hallock and Martha W. Raudabaugh, 31 July 1986.

[27] Personal interview with George W. Woodruff, 31 December 1985.

[28] *Daytona Beach News-Journal,* 27 March 1936.

Daytona Beach Sun Record, 18 February 1937.

[29] Personal interview with Jane Woodruff, 10 October 1986.

[30] Personal interview with George W. Woodruff, 23 July 1986.

[31] Telephone interview with Marie Beltin, 17 January 1987.

[32] Personal interview with George W. Woodruff, 27 May 1986.

[33] Personal interview with John A. Wallace, 25 August 1986.

[34] Personal interview with George W. Woodruff, 27 May 1986.

The Atlanta Journal and The Atlanta Constitution, 19 December 1971.

[35] Personal interview with George W. Woodruff, 27 May 1986.

[36] Personal interview with George W. Woodruff, 27 May 1986.

[37] Personal interview with Donn M. Gaebelein, 7 August 1986.

[38] Personal interview with George W. Woodruff, 27 May 1986.

The Highlander, Highlands, North Carolina, 4 April 1968.

[39] Personal interview with George W. Woodruff, 3 January 1986.

[40] Personal interview with Karl K. Anderson, 3 September 1986.

[41] Patsy Wilson, *A Time to Sow: Planting for the Lord,* (Privately published, 1978) 64.

[42] Ibid.

[43] Personal interview with George W. Woodruff, 3 January 1986.

[44] Personal interview with Karl K. Anderson, 14 September 1986.

Wilson, *A Time to Sow,* 62, 100, 102-105.

[45] Personal interview with Karl K. Anderson, 14 September 1986.

Wilson, *A Time to Sow,* 74.

[46] Personal interview with Karl K. Anderson, 14 September 1986.

[47] Ibid.

[48] Personal interview with Robert M. Hallock and Martha W. Raudabaugh, 31 July 1986.

[49] Personal interview with George W. Woodruff, 20 May 1986.

[50] Personal interview with George W. Woodruff, 31 December 1985.

Personal interview with Robert M. Hallock and Martha W. Raudabaugh, 31 July 1986.

[51] Ibid.

[52] Telephone interview with Charles L. Gowen, 13 September 1984.

[53]Personal interview with Joseph W. Jones, 3 October 1986.

Atlanta City Directory, 1924.

[54]Personal interview with Jane Woodruff, 10 October 1986.

[55]Ibid.

[56]Mary Frances Woodruff to Irene King Woodruff, 2 February 1942.

[57]*The Atlanta Journal*, Jane Woodruff's engagement announcement, n.d. (c. 1946).

[58]Personal interview with George W. Woodruff, 7 October 1986.

[59]Personal interview with James M. Sibley, 31 July 1986.

[60]Personal interview with George W. Woodruff, 7 October 1986.

[61]Personal interview with George L. Lanier, 15 October 1985.

[62]Personal interview with Charles L. Gowen, 4 August 1986.

[63]Personal interview with George W. Woodruff, 8 October 1986.

[64]Personal interview with John A. Wallace, 26 January 1987.

[65]Personal interview with George W. Woodruff, 8 October 1986.

The Valley Daily Times-News, 13 March 1951.

[66]Personal interview with John A. Wallace, 26 January 1987.

[67]Personal interview with Vela B. Rocker, George W. Woodruff's personal secretary 1959-1987, 29 May 1986. Also see personal interview with Joseph W. Jones, personal interview with Jane Woodruff, and personal interview with Hughes Spalding, Jr., 15 October 1985.

[68]Personal interview with Vela B. Rocker, 15 October 1985.

Also see personal interview with Joseph W. Jones, personal interview with Jane Woodruff, and personal interview with Hughes Spalding, Jr.

[69]Personal interview with James T. Laney, 7 August 1986.

[70]Personal interview with John A. Wallace, 25 August 1986.

[71]Personal interview with James T. Laney, 7 August 1986.

[72]Personal interview with John A. Wallace, 25 August 1986.

Personal interview with James M. Sibley, 31 July 1986.

[73]From the records of the corporate secretary of the Trust Company of Georgia.

[74]Personal interview with James B. Williams, 5 September 1986.

[75]Personal interview with James M. Sibley, 31 July 1986.

Personal interview with James B. Williams, 5 September 1986.

[76]Ibid.

[77]See personal interview with Donn M. Gaebelein; personal interview with James T. Laney; personal interview with Karl K. Anderson; personal interview with Ruth Schmidt, 20 August 30, 1986; personal interview with William L. Pressly, 11 August 1986; personal interview with R. Kirby Godsey, 25 August 1986; telephone interview with Joseph M. Pettit, 18 August 1986.

[78]Personal interview with Marie Beltin, 17 January 1987.

[79]Personal interview with Hughes Spalding, Jr., 15 October 1985.

[80]Franklin M. Garrett, *Atlanta and Its Environs: A Chronicle of Its People and Events*, 3 vols. (Athens, Georgia: University of Georgia Press, 1969) 2:641-42.

[81]Ibid.

[82] *The Atlanta Journal and Constitution Magazine,* 24 October 1965.

[83] Personal interview with Boisfeuillet Jones, 30 July 1986.

Charles Elliott, *"Mr. Anonymous": Robert Woodruff of Coca-Cola* (Atlanta: Cherokee Publishing Company, 1982) 149, 255-56.

[84] *The Atlanta Journal,* 19 August 1939.

[85] Elliott, *"Mr. Anonymous,"* 149.

[86] Personal interview with George W. Woodruff, 3 January 1986.

[87] Personal interview with Joseph W. Jones, 3 October 1986.

[88] Personal interview with George W. Woodruff, 3 January 1986.

[89] Telephone interview with Vela Rocker, 18 March 1987.

[90] Personal interview with James B. Williams, 5 September 1986.

Personal interview with George W. Woodruff, 3 January 1986.

Personal interview with James M. Sibley, 31 July 1986.

Personal interview with Boisfeuillet Jones, 30 July 1986.

[91] Personal interview with James M. Sibley, 31 July 1986.

Personal interview with James B. Williams, 5 September 1986.

[92] Personal interview with George W. Woodruff, 3 January 1986.

[93] Personal interview with Boisfeuillet Jones, 30 July 1986.

[94] Personal interview with James M. Sibley, 31 July 1986.

Personal interview with James B. Williams, 5 September 1986.

[95] Personal interview with George W. Woodruff, 3 January 1986.

Personal interview with Charles L. Gowen, 4 August 1986.

Personal interview with Hughes Spalding, Jr., 15 October 1985.

Personal interview with Boisfeuillet Jones, 30 July 1986.

[96] Personal interview with George W. Woodruff, 3 January 1986.

[97] *Emory Magazine,* May 1985.

[98] Personal interview with James B. Williams, 5 September 1986.

[99] Personal interview with James T. Laney, 7 August 1986.

Personal interview with Joseph W. Jones, 3 October 1986.

[100] Ibid.

[101] Personal interview with Vela Rocker, 15 October 1985.

[102] Personal interview with Boisfeuillet Jones, 30 July 1986.

[103] Personal interview with James T. Laney, 7 August 1986.

[104] *Emory Magazine,* May 1985.

[105] Personal interview with Dr. William C. McGarity, 6 August 1986.

[106] *DeKalb Extra,* 27 November 1980.

[107] Personal interview with Alfred D. Boylston, 30 July 1986.

[108] Manuscript tribute by Louise Inman Allen to Irene King Woodruff, Fall 1981, in the files of Jane Woodruff.

[109] *The Small Street Journal,* a quarterly publication of Henrietta Egleston Hospital for Children, Winter 1987.

[110] Personal interview with Warren Heemann, vice president for development, Georgia Institute of Technology, 1 October 1986.

Telephone interview with Pat McKenna, Secretary of The Georgia Tech Foundation, Inc., 17 March 1987.

[111]*TechTopics,* a publication of the Georgia Tech Alumni Association, April/May 1984.

[112]Personal interview with Warren Heemann, 1 October 1986.

[113]*TechTopics,* April/May 1984.

[114]Telephone interview with Bertie Bond, Agnes Scott College, 30 September 1986.

[115]Photographs of the Seven Mystic Maids are in Irene King Woodruff's personal collection, in the possession of her daughter, Jane Woodruff.

[116]*The Atlanta Constitution,* 23 November 1954.

Personal interview with Dr. Ruth Schmidt, President of Agnes Scott College, 6 August 1986.

[117]Walter Edward McNair, *Lest We Forget: An Account of Agnes Scott College* (Atlanta: Tucker-Castleberry Printing, Inc., 1983) 15.

[118]From the records of the secretary of Agnes Scott College.

[119]Garrett, *Atlanta,* 3:304.

[120]McNair, *Lest We Forget,* 151.

[121]Ibid., 151-54.

[122]News Release, 7 May 1975, Agnes Scott College News Service.

[123]Resolution of the Agnes Scott College Board of Trustees, adopted 11 October 1985, copy in George W. Woodruff's personal files in the possession of his daughter, Jane Woodruff.

[124]Personal interview with Donn M. Gaebelein, 7 August 1986.

[125]Personal interview with William L. Pressly, 11 August 1986.

[126]From The Westminster Schools admissions materials.

[127]Personal interview with George W. Woodruff, 3 January 1986.

Telephone interview with Jane Woodruff, 20 March 1987.

[128]Personal interview with Donn M. Gaebelein, 7 August 1986.

[129]From the Dedication of the Walter F. George Foundation Board Room.

[130]Personal interview with R. Kirby Godsey, 25 August 1986.

[131]Personal interview with Robert L. Steed, 25 September 1986.

[132]Mercer University News Release, 3 May 1979.

[133]Ibid.

[134]Ibid.

[135]Ibid.

[136]Mercer University News Release, 3 May 1979.

[137]Personal interview with Robert L. Steed, 25 September 1986.

[138]*The Mercerian,* Fall 1982.

[139]Personal interview with R. Kirby Godsey, 25 August 1986.

[140]Personal interview with Robert L. Steed, 25 September 1986.

Macon Telegraph & News, 8 May 1985.

[141]Personal interview with Robert L. Steed, 25 September 1986.

[142]Personal interview with Emily Myers, 7 October 1986.

[143]Remarks by Mercer President R. Kirby Godsey, 15 August 1984, at the unveiling of the George W. Woodruff bust.

[144]Griffin B. Bell and Robert L. Steed to George W. Woodruff, 13 October 1983.

[145] Personal interview with Robert M. Hallock and Martha W. Raudabaugh, 31 July 1986.

[146] Ibid.

[147] Personal interview with Jane Woodruff, 10 October 1986.

[148] Ibid.

[149] Personal interview with George W. Woodruff, 5 September 1985.

[150] Personal interview with James T. Laney, 7 August 1986.

Personal interview with William L. Pressly, 11 August 1986.

[151] Personal interview with James M. Sibley, 31 July 1986.

Personal interview with William L. Pressly, 11 August 1986.

Personal interview with Alfred D. Boylston, 30 July 1986.

[152] Personal interview with R. Kirby Godsey, 25 August 1986.

Personal interview with Emily Myers, 20 October 1986.

[153] Personal interview with R. Kirby Godsey, 25 August 1986.

[154] Personal interview with James M. Sibley, 31 July 1986.

Personal interview with Donn M. Gaebelein, 7 August 1986.

Personal interview with Emily Myers, 7 October 1986.

[155] Personal interview with Donn M. Gaebelein, 7 August 1986.

Bust of George W. Woodruff, commissioned by Mercer University and sculpted by Glenn Acree in 1984. The original of the bust is in the Woodruff House at Mercer University, and there are copies in the George W. Woodruff Library at The Westminster Schools, the George W. Woodruff Physical Education Center at Emory, Georgia Tech, and the Trust Company of Georgia.

Epilogue

On February 4, 1987, George Waldo Woodruff died at Emory University Hospital of pneumonia after a gradual decline in health over a period of several months. He was ninety-one.

Woodruff was mourned by his family and all he had touched in his many years of business leadership and philanthropy, and the support and enrichment that he had for so long provided to Egleston Hospital, Georgia Tech, Westminster, the Woodruff Medical Center at Emory University, Agnes Scott College, Rabun Gap-Nacoochee School, and the Walter F. George School of Law of Mercer University continued under the generous terms of his will.

Index

Acree, Glenn, artist commissioned to render bust of George Waldo Woodruff, 138, 145, 156
Agnes Scott College, 45, 135-137, 157
Allen, Ivan, Jr., 111, 133
Allen, Louise, 133
Alston, Wallace M., President of Agnes Scott College, 136
Alumni Distinguished Service Award (Georgia Tech), 135
American Society of Mechanical Engineers, 65
Anderson, Dr. Karl, 113
Atkinson, Harry M., 25
Atlanta Agricultural Works, 46-47
Atlanta Consolidated Street Railway Company, 24-26, 30
Atlanta Debutante Club, 118
Atlanta Ice & Coal Company, 29
Atlanta Plow Company, 47
Atlanta Railway & Power Company, 25
Atlanta Steel Company, 29-30
Atlanta Steel Hoop Company, 29-30
Atlanta, Georgia, 15, 35, 55, 59-60, 64, 71-72, 74, 82, 88, 101-102, 109, 113, 118, 121, 123, 130
   photographs, 21-22, 28-29, 44, 49, 82, 89, 118, 121, 123, 127, 131, 133-134, 137, 139
Atlantic Ice & Coal Company, 26, 29, 53, 83-84, 87-88, 105
Atlantic Steel Company, 53, 64, 82-83, 118, 143
Augusta National Golf Club, 110, 123
Avondale Grammar School, Birmingham, 104

Bailey, Albert H., 89
Balfour, Robert C., 122 (illus.)
Banks, William N., 127 (illus.)
Bates, Annie, 62
Bates, Maria Elizabeth Winship ("Aunt Lizzie"), 10, 38, 62
Bell, Griffin B., 142 (illus.), 145
Biltmore Hotel, Atlanta, 114

Bird, Angus E., 127 (illus.)
Bird, F. M., 127 (illus.)
Bird, Jay, 50
Birmingham Country Club, The, 102, 110
Birmingham Rotary Club, 102
Birmingham Trust and National Bank, 102
Bivings, Clara Belle King, 47, 49
Blackard, Dr. Embree H., 127 (illus.)
Bowden, Henry L., 127 (illus.)
Boylston, Alfred D., Jr., 111, 133
Branch, Harllee, Jr., 127 (illus.)
Burger, Warren E., 141, 142 (illus.)

Calhoun, Dr. F. Phinizy, 127 (illus.)
Callaham, Ed, 111 (illus.)
Cambridge, Massachusetts, 8, 58, 62
Campbell, J. B., 113
Candler, Asa Griggs, 47, 54, 84-86, 124-125
Candler, Charles Howard, Sr., 86, 127 (illus.)
Candler, C. Howard, Jr., 127 (illus.)
Candler, S. Charles, 127 (illus.)
Cantey, Morgan S., 127 (illus.)
Capital City Club, 35, 110
Carmichael, James V., 127 (illus.)
Carnegie Library (of Georgia Tech), 55
Carter, Hugh, 110
Central City Park (later renamed Woodruff Park), 130
Chase National Bank, 84, 86
Cleveland, President Grover, 10, 15
Cobb, Ty, 63
Coca-Cola Company, The, 87, 106, 123
   Candler, Asa Griggs, 47, 54, 84-86, 124-125
   Candler, Charles Howard, 86
   Coca-Cola International Corporation, medium through which the corpus of stock in the Ernest and Emily Woodruff Foundation was donated to Emory, 130

Coca-Cola stocks given to family as Christmas presents, 146
Dobbs, Samuel Candler, 54, 86
George Waldo Woodruff became active with The Coca-Cola Company, 118
gifts of Coca-Cola stock to Emory University, 127
growth of Coca-Cola stock, 126
Jacobs' Drug Store, first glass of Coca-Cola sold from this store's soda fountain, May, 1886, 84
Pemberton, John Styth, inventor of the base syrup for Coca-Cola, 84-85
product of the coca bean and the kola nut, 84
purchase of The Coca-Cola Company by Ernest Woodruff's syndicate for $25 million, 84-86
Robinson, Frank M., partner of John Styth Pemberton, 84
subsidiaries of The Coca-Cola Company, 119
Woodruff, Robert, took an active role in The Coca-Cola Company, 90
Coca-Cola Export Corporation, The 119
Coca-Cola Interamerican Corporation, 119
Coca-Cola, Ltd., Canada, 119
Coles, Cliff, 82
Columbia Pictures, 120
Columbus, Georgia, 4-6, 18, 31, 33-34
Comer, Donald S., 127 (illus.)
Commercial Travelers Savings Bank
founded by Joel Hurt, 122
later renamed Trust Company of Georgia, 25, 27, 122
Continental Gin Company, 115, 118, 120
company sold to Allied Products of Chicago in 1959, 147
following formation of corporation Thomas Elliott served as president until 1930, 99
manufacturer of the Eagle and Pratt Gins, 98
photographs, 100-102
Woodruff, George Waldo, elected president and chairman of the board, 99
Woodruff, George Waldo, moved his family to Birmingham, Alabama, to join management, 90
Woodruff, George Waldo, retired, 110
Woodruff, George Waldo, served as assistant to president in 1926, 97-98
Cornell University, Ithaca, New York, 55, 59
Country Club of Naples, The, Naples, Florida, 111
Cowan, Cecil B. ("Abie"), 116 (illus.)
Craft, George S., 127 (illus.)
Crawford, Perry, 111 (illus.)

Daugherty, Marshall, professor of art, Mercer University, who designed and executed the Woodruff Medal, 145
Daytona Beach, Florida, 106-108, 114
Daytona Country Club, 107, 110
Dean, F. S., 46
Deepdene Park, 47
Dellwood Park, 47
Dobbs, Samuel Candler, 54

Downing, Walter T., 21-22, 47
Druid Hills, Atlanta
area of Atlanta developed by Joel Hurt, 47
landscape architect and designer of Druid Hills, Frederick Law Olmstead, 47
section of Atlanta where Woodruff family resided, 114
Druid Hills Golf Club, Atlanta, 109-110
Dunham, Lucy Ariail (Mrs. Samuel Dunham), 4
Dunham, Samuel, 4

Eagle Gin Company, 98
Eagle Plain Gin, 98
East Lake Country Club, Atlanta, 109-110, 119
Edgewood Avenue School, Atlanta, 19-21, 32
Edgewood Street Railway Company, Atlanta, 24
Egleston Hospital for Children
donations of time and funds by George Waldo and Irene King Woodruff, 132-133, 157
founded in 1928 through posthumous grant of $100,000 from Thomas Egleston, 132
tribute to Irene King Woodruff by Louise Allen, 133
Elliott, Thomas, 98-99
Emily and Ernest Woodruff Chapel (Rabun Gap-Nacoochee School), 113
Emily W. Woodruff Administration Building (Rabun Gap-Nacoochee School), 113
Emory College
attended by Robert Woodruff, 32-33, 56
founded at Oxford, Georgia, in 1836, 124
moved to Atlanta and became Emory University, 124-125
Emory Medical Corps
George Waldo Woodruff joined in 1918, 73
Emory University
campaign for Emory of 1979, 128
Candler, Asa Griggs, famous "Million Dollar Letter" as incentive for Emory College to relocate in Atlanta, 125
corpus of Ernest and Emily Woodruff Fund in the form of stock in the Coca-Cola International Corporation in 1980, 127, 130, 145
Emory College became two-year liberal arts college on new Atlanta campus, 125
established Schools of Medicine, Dentistry, Nursing, Theology, Law, and Business, and the Graduate School of Arts and Sciences, 125
George and Irene Woodruff Residential Center, 132
George Waldo Woodruff Physical Education Center, athletic complex designed by John Portman, 130, 131 (illus.)
Laney, James T., 128, 130-132
list of Board of Trustees as of January, 1957, 127 (illus.)
photograph of Board of Trustees taken January, 1957, 127
Robert Winship Memorial Clinic for treatment of cancer established by the Ernest and Emily Woodruff Foundation, 125

strongly supported by Woodruff family, 126, 157
Emory University, Trustees: William N. Banks, Angus E. Bird, F. M. Bird, Dr. Embree H. Blackard, Henry L. Bowden, Harllee Branch, Jr., Dr. F. Phinizy Calhoun, C. Howard Candler, Jr., Charles Howard Candler, Sr., S. Charles Candler, Morgan S. Cantey, James V. Carmichael, Donald S. Comer, George S. Craft, Aubrey F. Folts, Bishop Marvin A. Franklin, Dr. Wadley R. Glenn, Granger Hansell, Dr. Noland Harmon, Jr., Dr. Luther A. Harrell, Senator Spessard L. Holland, James C. Malone, Harry Y. McCord, Jr., L. P. McCord, Bishop Arthur J. Moore, James D. Robinson, Dr. Lester A. Rumble, Charles M. Trammell, William B. Turner, Bishop William T. Watkins, Dr. Goodrich White, 127 (illus.)
Emory University Hospital, 130, 146, 157
Empire Mills, Columbus, 5-6, 10
Equitable Building, Atlanta, built by Joel Hurt, 26-28
Eubanks, Sarah, 38

Faulkes, Lillian, 106 (illus.)
Ferrall, Jim, 58
First National Bank and Trust Company of Augusta, 123
First Presbyterian Church, Atlanta, 118
Five Points, Atlanta, section of the city that includes Central City Park, renamed Woodruff Park in 1985, 24, 26, 28 (illus.), 32
Folts, Aubrey F., 127 (illus.)
Fort McPherson, 72-73
Franklin, Bishop Marvin A., 127 (illus.)

George Waldo Woodruff Medal of Excellence (Mercer University), 145
Gaebelein, Donn, 111, 137-138
General Pipe and Foundry Company, 33, 56, 87
George and Irene Woodruff Community Center (Highlands, N. C.), 112
George Waldo Woodruff Dormitory (Rabun Gap-Nacoochee School), 113
George Waldo Woodruff Library (The Westminster Schools), 138
George Waldo Woodruff Physical Education Center, (Emory University), 130, 131 (illus.)
Georgia Military Academy, 32
Georgia Power Company, 47
Georgia School of Technology, 34
Georgia Tech, 32, 38, 43, 50, 52, 56, 58, 60, 64, 72, 82, 98, 145
    Alumni Association Thousand Club Award bestowed upon George Waldo Woodruff, 135
    Carnegie Library, 35
    Grant Field, also known as Tech Flats by students, 35
    Irene and George Woodruff Dormitory built in 1984, 135
    Joseph Brown Whitehead Hospital, 35
    Kappa Alpha Chapter in which George W. Woodruff held membership in 1914, 35-37
    Lyman Hall Chemistry Lab, 35
    photographs, 35, 37, 44, 53-54
    Woodruff, George Waldo, entered as freshman in 1913 to study mechanical engineering, 34
    Woodruff, George Waldo, left Tech for a northeastern school, 55
Georgia Tech Foundation, The, 134
Glenn, Mrs. Thomas, 116 (illus.)
Glenn, Thomas K., 63, 82-83, 116 (illus.), 143
Glenn, Dr. Wadley R., 127 (illus.)
Goddard, John N., 155 (illus.)
Goddard, Mrs., J. N., 116 (illus.)
Golf, East Lake Country Club, 109-110, 119
Goodrum, Mrs. Jim, 116 (illus.)
Gowen, Charles, 119
Grady Hospital, 125
Grady, Henry W., 15
Graham-Eckes School, Daytona Beach, 108, 114, 118
Guaranty Trust Company of New York
    Eugene Stetson, President and Chairman of the Board, 63
    participation in the purchase of The Coca-Cola Company by Ernest Woodruff from the Candler family, 84, 86
Gulf Stream Country Club, Delray Beach, 107, 110

Halifax River, Florida, 108
Hallock, Dorothy Nell, 146
Hallock, George Woodruff, 146
Hallock, Martha Virginia ("Missie"), 146
Hallock, Robert M., Jr., 146
Hallock, Robert Monroe, 91, 118, 146
    member, Alpha Tau Omega Fraternity, University of Florida, Gainesville, 114
Hallum, Basil, 9
Hansell, Granger, 127 (illus.)
Hard Bargain Cottage, 5
Harmon, Dr. Noland, Jr., 127 (illus.)
Harrell, Dr. Luther A., 127 (illus.)
Harris, Lucy, 89, 104
Harris, Dr. Rufus, 140-141
Harrison, Julian, 111
Hayes, Ralph, 116
Highlands Country Club, The, Highlands, North Carolina, 108-110, 114
Highlands Cashiers Hospital, 112
Hurt, Annie Bright Woodruff (Mrs. Joel Hurt), 5, 7, 23, 33
Hurt, Joel
    born 1850, died 1926, 24
    brother-in-law to Ernest Woodruff, 7, 10-11, 23
    builder of the Equitable Building, Atlanta, in 1891, 26-27
    convinced Ernest Woodruff to move his family to Atlanta from Columbus in 1893, 10-11, 18, 23-25
    developed and resided in Inman Park, 24, 33

developer of Druid Hills in Atlanta, 47
founded Commercial Savings Travelers Savings Bank, later renamed Trust Company of Georgia, 11, 25, 27, 122
founded Edgewood Street Railway Company in 1886, Atlanta, 24
married Annie Bright Woodruff in 1876 at family home in Columbus, 7, 24
photograph, 24
Hurt, Sherwood, 18, 19, 21, 26
Hutchings, Drucella Bonner (Mrs. Robert Hutchings), 8
Hutchings, Robert, 8

Ichauway Plantation, 122
Inman Park
developed and resided in by Joel Hurt, 24, 33
Downing, Walter T., 21-22
Edgewood Avenue School renamed Inman Park School, Atlanta, 19, 21, 32
elite residential area of Atlanta circa 1910, 47
home of Ernest and Emily Woodruff, 22 (illus.), 23, 30
Insurance Company of North America, 139-141
Irene King Woodruff Fund (Egleston Hospital), 133
Irene King Woodruff Hall (Rabun Gap-Nacoochee School), 113-114

Jones, Bobby, 109-110
Jones, Elizabeth Hurt, 23
Jordan, Henry, 108-109
Joseph Brown Whitehead Hospital, Georgia Tech, 35

Kappa Alpha Fraternity, 35, 36-37 (illus.), 49, 52, 53 (illus.), 58
Kelley, Gene, 116 (illus.)
King & Spalding, 120, 141
King Hardware Store, 43
King home
274 Ponce de Leon Avenue, later renumbered as 430, 43, 45-47, 49, 105
Alpha Delta Pi Sorority, 79
King's Inn, Highlands, North Carolina, 114
King, Bobby, 114
King, Clara Belle, 78, 46 (illus.), 92 (illus.), 105 (illus.)
King, Jr., Clyde L., 92 (illus.)
King, Clyde Lanier
became ill, 114
born in 1875, 43
died in 1941, 118
father of Irene Tift King Woodruff, 43
home of, 274 Ponce de Leon Avenue, later renumbered 430, moved in circa 1894, 45, 46 (illus.), 47
home of, 1010 Ponce de Leon Street, later renumbered 1386, circa 1911, 46-47, 49 (illus.), 61, 79
Irene and George Woodruff's wedding invitation, 75 (illus.)
married Clara Belle Rushton, June 1894, 45

photographs, 46, 92, 105
King, Frances Poole (Mrs. Clyde L. King, Jr.), 92 (illus.)
King, George, 43
King, John, 47, 78, 92 (illus.), 105
King, John Woodruff, 146
King, Martha Anderson (Mrs. James Lawrence King), 43
King, Reverend James Lawrence, 43
King, Richard W., 91, 118, 146
member, Alpha Tau Omega Fraternity, University of Florida, Gainesville, 114
King-Smith Studio School, Washington, D. C., 114

Laney, James T., 128, 130, 131 (illus.), 132
Lanier, Joseph L., 119-120
Ledsinger, Lewis, 50
Lindsay, Elizabeth Bright Cooper (Mrs. Sherwood Conner Lindsay), 5
Lindsay, Sherwood Conner, 5
Logan, Harold S., 142
Lowndes, Dr. Richard H., 34
Lummus Gin Company, Columbus, 102

Maiden, Stewart, 109
Malone, James C., 127 (illus.)
Marietta, Georgia, 31
Massachusetts Institute of Technology, 56 (illus.), 57, 62-65, 73, 80
excerpt of letter to George Woodruff from his mother, Emily, 59
threat of war in Europe became a significant factor to George Woodruff during the school year 1916, 69-72
Woodruff, George Waldo, credited M.I.T. for much of his ability and success as a businessman, 98
Woodruff, George Waldo, enrolled as student in 1916, 56
Matheson, Kenneth Gordon, 34
Mayer, Hazel, 79 (illus.)
McCord, Jr., Harry Y., 127 (illus.)
McCord, L. P., 127 (illus.)
McGarity, Dr. William C., 132
McGovern, Frank, 116 (illus.)
McKenzie, Catherine, 106 (illus.)
Melton, Buckner, 144
Mercer University
George Waldo Woodruff Medal of Excellence awarded annually to law student with highest average, 145
interior design, decoration, and furnishings of Woodruff house provided by Doris Moughon Schuler of Birmingham, Alabama, 145
located in Macon, Georgia, 139
obtained the Insurance Company of North America building on Coleman Hill which is now the Walter F. George School of Law, 139-142, 144-145
site of the Woodruff House and the Sibley Institute of Public Affairs, 138-140, 142, 144-145
Steed, Robert L., instrumental in acquisition of the

Woodruff House and Insurance Company of North America building, 140-42, 144
    Walter F. George School of Law, 139-142, 144-145, 157
Mesherel, John, 4
Mesherel, Polly Smith (Mrs. John Mesherel), 4
Michael, Alfred Benjamin, Jr., 91, 145
    member, Alpha Tau Omega Fraternity, University of Florida, Gainesville, 114
Michael, Irene Woodruff, 145-146
Monie, George W. Woodruff's Chris Craft Cruiser, 107 (illus.), 114-115
Moore, Bishop Arthur J., 127 (illus.)
Morgan, George, 100
Mount Vernon Junior College, 118
Munger Gin and Machine Company, 98
Munger, Northington, Pratt Gin Co., 98
Munger, Robert S., 98
Murray Gin Company, Dallas, 102

National Park Seminary, Forest Glen, Maryland, 51-52 (illus.), 76, 79 (illus.)
    photographs of Irene King Woodruff, while at school, 61-62
    school attended by Irene King Woodruff, 50-52, 60-62
    Woodruff, Irene King graduated in 1918, 73
Newell, Alfred, 116 (illus.)

Oak Grove Park, 47
Olmstead, Frederick Law, 47
Ordinance Department U. S. Army, 73
Overby, Asenath Caroline Thrasher, 9
Overlook Mansion (now the Woodruff House, Mercer University), 142

Palmetto Club, Daytona Beach, 106
Parker, William, 111
Peachtree Golf Club, Atlanta, 110-111
Pemberton, John Styth, 84-85
Piedmont Driving Club, 15, 30, 35
Piedmont Park, Atlanta, 15, 16 (illus.)
Powell, J. E., 46
Pratt Double Rib Huller Gin, 98
Pratt Gin Company, 98
Pressly, Dr. William L., 137-138
Rabun Gap-Nacoochee School
    Dr. Karl Anderson, president from 1936 until 1984, 113
    devotion of George and Irene Woodruff to Rabun Gap Nacoochee School, 157
    Emily W. Woodruff Administration Building, 113
    formed in 1928 through merger of Rabun Gap Industrial School and Nacoochee Institute, 112
    George W. Woodruff Dormitory, 113
    Irene King Woodruff Hall, dormitory dedicated in 1976, 113, 114 (illus.)
    Karl Anderson Hall, residence hall dedicated in 1976, 114 (illus).

located near Helen, Georgia, 112
Reid, Neel, 47
Ritchie, Dr. Andrew, 112
Robinson, Frank M., 84
Robinson, James D., Jr., 127 (illus.)
Robuck Golf Club, Birmingham, 102, 110
Rossignol, Charles P., 80
Ruffner, General Clark L., 111
Ruffwood, Highlands, North Carolina, 108-110, 112
Rumble, Dr. Lester A., 127 (illus.)
Rushton, Ella Byron Wight (Mrs. Robert E. Rushton), 43, 45 (illus.)
Rushton family home, Capitol Avenue, 45
Rushton, Robert Ellwood, 9, 43, 45

Samford, Frank P., 120
Saul, Ralph S., 142 (illus.)
Schmidt, Dr. Ruth A., 134 (illus.)
Schuler, Doris Moughon, 145
Schwarzman, Dr. Stephen W., 132
Seabreeze Country Club, Daytona Beach, 107, 110
Shutze, Philip, 47
Sibley Horticulture Building, Callaway Gardens, 143
Sibley Institute of Public Affairs, Mercer University, 140, 142, 144
Sibley, John Adams, 111, 141
    partner in Spalding, Sibley, Troutman & Kelley now known as King & Spalding, 120
    photographs, 140, 143-144
    Sibley Horticulture Building at Callaway Gardens, 143
    Sibley Institute for Public Affairs housed in the Woodruff House at Mercer University, 140, 142, 144
    Trust Company of Georgia, Chairman of the Board, 139, 143
Simmons, William P., 140
Smith, Ed, 111
Smith, Ephraim, 3
Smith, Rachel Cole (Mrs. Ephraim Smith), 3
Sowersby, Phil, 111 (illus.)
Springdale Park, 47
Steed, Robert L., 140-42, 144-45
Steel, Harry, 28
Stetson, Eugene, 63
Stevens, Peter, artist commissioned in 1970 to paint portrait of George W. Woodruff; original currently hangs in the Walter F. George School of Law (with a copy in the Woodruff House), 129 (illus.)
Strickland, Robert, 116 (illus.), 143

Talmadge, Governor Eugene, 115
Tech High (Atlanta, Georgia), 32, 34, 82, 98
Terry Shipbuilding Company, Savannah, 74, 82
Trammell, Charles M., 127 (illus.)
Troutman, Robert, 120
Trust Company of Georgia
    bank president, Jimmy Williams, chaired the 1979

Campaign for Emory, 128
fiftieth anniversary of company in September, 1941, 117
founded in 1891 by Joel Hurt under the name of the Commercial Travelers Savings Bank, 25, 27, 122
involvement of Ernest Woodruff, 26
John Sibley, Chairman of the Board, 1951, 120, 139, 143
photographs, 29, 117, 123, 143
purchase of Atlantic Steel holdings by syndicate formed by Ernest Woodruff, 64
renamed in fall of 1893, 27
role in purchase of The Coca-Cola Company by Woodruff syndicate, 84
successor to Ernest Woodruff first as president then chairman of the board, Tom Glenn, 63
Turner, William B., 127 (illus.)

Uncas ("Tunxis") Sepos, 3
University of Florida, Gainesville, 114

Virgile Park, 47

Walter F. George Foundation, 140-141, 143, 145
Walter F. George School of Law, 129, 139-141
Walters, Drury, 116
Walters, George, 31
Walters, Mary Frances Winship, 31, 116 (illus.)
Wardlaw, Billy, 111
Washington Seminary (predecessor to The Westminster Schools), Atlanta, graduates include Clara Belle King, Irene Woodruff and Jane Woodruff, 118, 138
Watkins, Bishop William T., 127 (illus.)
Watlington, Fannie, 79 (illus.)
Wesleyan Female College, 45
West Point Manufacturing Company, 119
West Point-Pepperell, Inc., 119, 121 (illus.)
Westminster Schools, The
  Gaebelein, Donn, President, 111, 137-138
  George Waldo Woodruff Library dedicated September 1985, houses bust of Woodruff commissioned by Mercer University, 138, 145, 156
  Irene and George Woodruff Elementary School dedicated 1981, 138
  origin is merger of the North Avenue Presbyterian School, renamed Napsonian School, with Washington Seminary, 138
  photograph, 137
  Woodruff, George Waldo, devotion to, 138, 157
Westmoreland, Johnny, 110
White Motor Company
  place of employment for Robert Woodruff, 52, 54, 61, 87-88, 90
  White, Walter, owner of the White Motor Company, 54, 88
White, Bob, 110
White, Dr. Goodrich, 127 (illus.)
White, Walter, 54, 88

Wiard, John, 4
Wiard, Phebe Hurlbut (Mrs. John Wiard), 4
Wickersham, Charles A., 31
Wightsville, Georgia, 45
Wild Cat Cliffs Club, Highlands, North Carolina, 110
Williams, Jimmy, 30, 123, 128
Winship, Anne, 10
Winship, Benjamin, 8
Winship, Charles Robert, 10
Winship, Edward, 7-8
Winship, Edward II, 8, 62
Winship, Edward III, 8
Winship, Elizabeth (Mrs. Edward Winship I), 8
Winship, Emily Hutchings (Mrs. Joseph Winship), 8-9
Winship, Frances, 79 (illus.)
Winship, George, 9, 45
Winship, Hannah (Mrs. Isaac Winship), 8
Winship, Isaac, 8-9
Winship, Joseph, 8
Winship Machine Company, 9-10, 45, 98
Winship, Mary Adams (Mrs. Benjamin Winship), 8
Winship, Mary Frances Overby (Mrs. Robert Winship), 7, 9, 10 (illus.), 17, 19, 23
Winship, Rebecca Barsham (Mrs. Edward Winship II), 8, 62
Winship, Robert, 7, 9, 10 (illus.), 19-20, 23
Winship, Sarah Manning (Mrs. Edward Winship III), 8
Woderoue, Robert, 2
Woderove, John, 2
Wolbach, William W., 120
Woodroffe, David, 2
Woodroffe, John, 2
Woodroffe, Sir Nicholson, 2
Woodroufe, John, 2
Woodruff, Alzara, 4
Woodruff, Ashbel, 4
Woodruff, Charles Henry, 4
Woodruff, Daniel, 3
Woodruff, Diadamia Dunham (Mrs. George Wyllys Woodruff, George's second wife), 4
Woodruff, Emily Caroline Winship (Mrs. Ernest Woodruff), 20, 45, 53, 60, 72, 106
  born in 1867, second of five children, to parents Robert and Mary Frances Winship, 10
  celebrated fiftieth wedding anniversary with husband Ernest on April 22, 1935, 116
  created the Emily and Ernest Woodruff Foundation, 125
  died of cancer August of 1939 at age of 72, 114
  married Ernest Woodruff, April 22, 1885, 7
  mother of four sons, Robert Winship, Ernest, Jr. (who died at age 3), George Waldo, and Henry Francis, 10-11, 18
  moved with husband Ernest and youngest son, Henry, to Maidens, Virginia, 115
  nicknamed "Monie" by grandchildren, 105
  owned an electric car, 31

photographs, 22, 31, 73, 75, 77, 82, 116
returned to Atlanta, 116
support for Rabun Gap-Nacoochee School, 112-113
traveled to Boston and New York to visit George and to see shows, 62

Woodruff, Ernest, 23, 31, 52-53, 55-56, 58, 60, 64, 70, 71-73, 75, 97, 104-105, 115, 122, 126
arranged syndicate to purchase The Coca-Cola Company from Candler family for $25 million, 84
assisted son, George Waldo, with securing position with Terry Shipbuilding in Savannah, 74
became ill, 114
born third son to George Waldo and Virginia Woodruff in 1863, 5
bought first car in Atlanta, 30
celebrated golden wedding anniversary with Emily on April 22, 1930, at White Sulpher Springs, West Virginia, 116
description of formation of Woodruff syndicate in 1919 which enabled the purchase of The Coca-Cola Company, 86
died in 1944 at the age of 81, 118
director on the board of Atlantic Ice & Coal, 26, 88
father of four sons, Robert Winship, Ernest, Jr. (who died at age 3), George Waldo, and Henry Francis, 10-11, 18
formed the Emily and Ernest Woodruff Foundation in 1937 at the suggestion of their sons, Robert and George, 125
married Emily Caroline Winship, April 22, 1885, 7
named vice president then president of Atlanta Consolidated Street Railway, 24-26, 29-30
nickname given to Ernest by grandchildren "Pa" 105
photographs, 77, 87, 116-117
provided his sons with a strong emphasis on careful accounting and good stewardship of financial resources, 59
recruited son, George, to join the Continental Gin Company located in Birmingham, Alabama, in a management position, 90
recruited son, Robert, to join The Coca-Cola Company in a management position, 90
support of Rabun Gap-Nacoochee School, 112-113
urged by brother-in-law, Joel Hurt, to move to Atlanta, 10-11, 18, 23-25
visited his son, George Waldo, at Massachusetts Institute of Technology, 62-63
worked at Empire Mills for 10 years, 5-6, 10

Woodruff Foundation, Emily and Ernest, 143
assisted in funding purchase of Insurance Company of North America Building for Law School, 139-141
corpus of foundation renamed Emily and Ernest Woodruff Fund transferred to Emory at a value of $105 million, now valued at $250 million, 127-128, 130
establishment of Emily and Ernest Woodruff Foundation, 125

foundation support for Georgia Tech, 134-135
foundation support for Rabun Gap-Nacoochee School, Agnes Scott College, Mercer University and The Westminster Schools, 136-139, 141-142
foundation's role in the establishment of the Robert Winship Memorial Clinic at Emory, 125
funded purchase of Overlook Mansion in Macon, renamed The Woodruff House of Mercer University, 142, 144-145
substantial source of support and growth for Emory for over forty years, 126

Woodruff, Francis, 5-6
Woodruff, George Sherwood, 5
Woodruff, George Waldo I, 4-6, 11
Woodruff, George Wyllys, 4-5
Woodruff golden wedding anniversary, 116
Woodruff, Hannah (Mrs. Matthew Woodruff), 3
Woodruff, Henry Francis, 18-19, 21, 23, 31 (illus.), 116 (illus.), 126 (illus.)
Woodruff, Henry Lindsay, 5, 34
Woodruff House, The, at Mercer University, 140 (illus.), 142, 144 (illus.), 145, 156
Woodruff, Irene King, 105, 133
attended Avondale Grammar School in Birmingham, 104
attended Graham-Eckes School in Daytona, 108
attended King-Smith Studio School for artists in Washington, D. C., 114
began piano lessons in Birmingham, continued in Daytona Beach, after move there, 104, 108
first child born to George and Irene Woodruff on November 8, 1918, 89
married Alfred Benjamin Michael, Jr., on June 26, 1940, 91, 114, 145
mother of one daughter, Irene Woodruff Michael, 145-146
moved with family to 212 Lullwater Road from 104 Oakdale Road in 1925, 89 (illus.), 90
moved with family to Birmingham in 1926, 90
moved with family from Birmingham to Daytona Beach, 106
photographs, 91-92, 104, 106, 108
spent summer vacations in Highlands, and Sapphire, North Carolina, 113

Woodruff, Irene Tift King, 17, 55-56, 70, 76, 84, 88-89
attended National Park Seminary in Forest Glen, Maryland, 30, 37, 60-61, 63
became mother to three daughters, Irene King, Mary Frances, and Jane, 89
bequeathed $1 million to Agnes Scott College to endow returning student program, 137
born April 16, 1898, as first child of Clyde and Clara Belle King, 43
bought an English Tudor home at 3668 Tuxedo Road when they moved back to Atlanta, 116, 135, 146
corresponded with George Waldo Woodruff while both

attended school, 52-57, 60-61, 63-65, 69, 71
donated both time and funds to Egleston Hospital for Children, 133
during attendance at National Park Seminary studied for Red Cross certification because of threat of war, 72
first home, 274 Ponce de Leon Avenue, later renumbered as 430, 45-46
funds donated to Highlands-Cashiers Hospital used to build the George and Irene Woodruff Community Center, 112
George Woodruff built summer home in Highlands, North Carolina for the family named "Ruffwood," 109 (illus.)
graduated from National Park Seminary, 73
married George Waldo Woodruff on April 17, 1918, 74, 78-80
moved into house at 104 Oakdale Road in Druid Hills in 1923, 89
met George Waldo Woodruff at age of 17, 47
moved with family to 1010 Ponce de Leon Avenue (later renumbered as 1386), in 1926, 47
moved with husband and daughters into new home at 212 Lullwater Road, 90
moved with husband and daughters to Birmingham, 98, 102
moved with husband and daughters to Daytona Beach in 1933, 106
nicknamed "Sweetie" by grandchildren, 146
photographs, 46, 48, 51, 52, 53, 54, 57, 61-62, 75, 77, 79, 81, 82, 89, 91-92, 104, 106, 108-110, 114, 118
siblings include two brothers, Clyde and John, and a sister, Clara Belle, 47
spent honeymoon in New York City, 80
spent summers vacationing in Highlands, North Carolina, 108
Woodruff, Jane, 105, 115, 133
attended Mount Vernon Junior College, graduated in 1945, 118
attended Washington Seminary, 138
began piano lessons, 108
born on September 30, 1925, 89
children, two sons Richard Woodruff King and John Woodruff King, 146
member of Atlanta Debutante Club, 118
moved soon after birth from Oakdale Road to 212 Lullwater Road, Atlanta, 90
moved to Birmingham in 1926 with parents, 104
moved with family to Daytona Beach in 1933, 106
parents, Irene and George Woodruff, 89
photographs, 91, 92, 104, 106, 108
summer holidays spent in Highlands, and Sapphire, North Carolina, 108, 113
Woodruff, Jonathan, 3
Woodruff, Jr., Ernest, 18
Woodruff, Lucy Mesherel (Mrs. George Wyllys Woodruff), 4
Woodruff, Lydia Smith (Mrs. Daniel Woodruff), 3
Woodruff, Mary Frances, 133, 135
attended Avondale Grammar School in Birmingham, 104
attended Graham-Eckes School in Daytona Beach, 108
born April 22, 1923, second daughter to Irene and George Woodruff, 89
graduated 1942 Mount Vernon Junior College, Washington, D. C., 118
married Robert M. Hallock in 1943, later divorced, 91, 118, 146
member of Atlanta Debutante Club, 118
mother of four children, Robert M., Jr., George Woodruff, Martha Virginia ("Missie"), and Dorothy Nell, 146
moved with family from Atlanta to Birmingham in 1926, 104
moved with family from Birmingham to Daytona Beach in 1933, 106
moved 1925 with family from 104 Oakdale Road to 212 Lullwater Road, 89 (illus.), 90
photographs, 91-92, 104, 106, 108
spent summers in Highlands, and Sapphire, North Carolina, 108, 113
Woodruff, Matthew, 2, 3
Woodruff, Nell Hodgson (Mrs. Robert Woodruff), 52-53, 61, 71-72, 116 (illus.)
Woodruff, origins and variations of the name, 2
Woodruff, Phebe Wiard (Mrs. Jonathan Woodruff), 4
Woodruff, Rebecca Clark (Mrs. Samuel Woodruff), 3
Woodruff, Robert Winship, 28, 31, 33, 53, 56, 60, 63, 71-72, 77, 113, 128, 130
attended Edgewood Avenue School, 20
attended Emory College, Oxford, Georgia, 32, 56
attended Georgia Military Academy, renamed Woodward Academy, 32
born in 1889 as first son to Ernest and Emily Woodruff, 10
changed his official residence to Wilmington, Delaware, in connection with corporate tax laws, 115
commissioned as captain in January of 1918 in the Ordinance Department U. S. Army, 73
employed at General Pipe and Foundry Company, 56
employed by White Motor Company, 61, 87
established the Emily and Ernest Woodruff Foundation with his brother, George Waldo Woodruff, in 1937, 125
grew up in home at 908 Edgewood Avenue, later renumbered as 708, 22
Ichauway Plantation in south Georgia used for hunting purchased in the 1940's, 122
involvement in purchase of The Coca-Cola Company, 86
married Nell Hodgson, 52
moved back to Atlanta in 1946, 116

INDEX

moved with family from Columbus to Atlanta in 1893, 18
photographs, 33, 116-117, 121-122, 126
persuaded by his father to leave White Motor Company and become manager of The Coca-Cola Company, 90
purchased fleet of trucks at cost from White Motor Company while employed there, 88
served as a director of Trust Company of Georgia, 122

Woodruff, Samuel, 3
Woodruff, Sybil Ingraham (Mrs. Ashbel Woodruff), 4
Woodruff, Virginia Bright Lindsay (Mrs. George Waldo Woodruff I), 5-6, 33
Woodruff, Virginia Lee, 5
Woolfolk, Kate, 79 (illus.)
Wyatt, Sir Frances, 8

Yates, Charlie, 111
Yellowstone National Park, 32

Zellars, John, 141

Mercer University, Law School, Macon, Georgia, 15 September 1986.